# Re-Calling Ministry

# Re-Calling Ministry

## JAMES E. DITTES
### Edited by Donald Capps

Chalice Press®
St. Louis, Missouri

Bible quotations, unless otherwise noted, are from the *New Revised Standard Version Bible,* copyright 1989, Division of Christian Education of the National Council of Churches of Christ in the USA. Used by permission. All rights reserved.

Those quotations marked RSV are from the *Revised Standard Version of the Bible,* copyright 1952 [2nd edition, 1971] by the Division of Christian Education of the National Council of the Churches of Christ in the United States of America. Used by permission. All rights reserved.

"Who Am I That I Should Go," "38 Years on the Verge," "Administration vs. Ministry," and "Preaching as Risky Investment" originally appeared in *Minister on the Spot* (Pilgrim Press, 1970). "Ministry as Grief Work," "Ministry: In Place, No Place," "Seeing Through Expectations to Find Ministry," "Counseling in the Wilderness," and "Shepherding Programs or Getting Lost Together?" were originally published in *When The People Say No* (Harper and Row, 1979). "The Empty Yes and the Masked Yes," "Confessions of the Golden Calf," "Joseph: Frozen Power," and "Joseph: Called into Service," were originally published in *The Male Predicament* (Harper and Row, 1985). "Modern Josephs: A Powerful Sense of Presence" is excerpted from "The Mitigated Self," in R. K. Fenn and D. Capps, eds., *The Endangered Self* (Princeton Theological Seminary, 1992).

Cover design: Michael Domínguez
Cover art: "The Tightrope Walker" by Paul Klee. Guggenheim Museum, New
        York City. Used by permission.
Art director: Michael Domínguez
Interior design: Elizabeth Wright

Visit Chalice Press on the World Wide Web at
www.chalicepress.com

10 9 8 7 6 5 4 3 2 1                                    99 00 01 02 03 04

**Library of Congress Cataloging–in–Publication Data**

Dittes, James E.
    Re-calling ministry / by James E. Dittes: edited by Donald Capps.
        p.   cm.
    ISBN 0-8272-3217-9
    1. Clergy—Religious life.   2. Clergy—Office.   I. Capps, Donald.    II. Title.
    BV4011.6.D58    1999                                                99-38565
    253—dc21                                                                CIP

Printed in the United States of America

**Recall**: v. 1. To summon (a person) to return. 2. To bring back into the mind, to recollect, to remember. 3. To call back (a product) for remedy or renewal. 4. To dislodge (from office) by a people's directive. 5. To summon anew.

# Contents

# Editor's Preface

James E. Dittes, Professor of Pastoral Theology and Professor of Psychology at Yale University, is a wise and gifted man. He has touched, strengthened, and deepened the lives of many through his teaching, his writings, and his personal being. Unlike those who insist on their right to speak, who demand to be heard, he is a man who does not force himself upon others but instead practices "the art of making space for others to grow." Unlike those who strive and compete for influence, who jockey for power and recognition, he stands for the power that comes from yielding the floor to others. Throughout a career manifesting the multiple identities of teacher, counselor, scientific researcher, journal editor, author, department head, professional society president, advocate for institutional reform—there is one identity that has held all of this multiplicity together and kept it grounded, the identity of a minister of the gospel. Keenly aware of his brilliant mind and depth of learning and insight, students of his have been awed—and inspired—that he has chosen not to write texts that parade learning but passionate, self-involving meditations on the minister and the predicaments and pressures that are endemic to faithful ministry.

In one of the chapters of this book, he gives moving testimony to his grandfather who, after a successful ministry in his thirties, responded to his denomination's request to move West and start a new church. But once he had moved, denominational support was not forthcoming, leaving him stranded and a failure: "Now off the career ladder, stigmatized, shunted aside by church officials guilty over their own miscalculation, he was unable for years to find another church, and then never one able to fully require or appreciate his talents." He never complained, however, until late in his life, "when the houselights suddenly came up on the Psalms he had been reading...and he noticed that they were true, that the wicked had prospered and that he hadn't...Bitterness escaped from him in the form of his warning to me: 'Take a good look down the road before you make any big decisions.'" Others might have chided the older man for giving vent to bitterness. Not Dittes. Instead, he asked, "Why can't mentors pass on this hard-won wisdom...this wisdom that the roles of ministers are isolated roles, not part of a genuine working ecology?" The meditations on ministry presented here are such hard-won wisdom. They have helped—and will continue to help—colleagues in ministry work through their own gardens of Gethsemane, their own griefs of betrayal.

The chapters in this book are selected (with one exception) from the following books: *Minister on the Spot*, *When the People Say No: Conflict and the Call to Ministry*, and *The Male Predicament*. James Dittes gave unstintingly of his time and energy toward the book's realization, making invaluable suggestions regarding chapters for inclusion, and has revised each chapter with a contemporary readership in mind. There is a sense, however, in which these chapters were already fully and richly contemporary, for he was far ahead of his time when these books were originally written (1970 to 1985), concerned then, as now, with predicaments and pressures that are endemic to ministry, whenever, wherever, and by whomever it occurs.

The original sources for each chapter are listed on the copyright page. I would especially note that the selections from *The Male Predicament* were originally written as analyses of typical experiences of ministers. At the insistence of the original publisher's editors, however, the manuscript was revised to reflect a more general application to all men, not ministers only; though, as the prologue to the present book reflects, considerable illustrative material relating to ministry survived this change in focus. In the present volume, these chapters have been restored essentially to their original, prepublication form.

The genesis of this book has been one of the great satisfactions of my own ministerial career. It has led me to recall and reexperience my own first readings of these texts. Now, as then, they recall the astonishment of the two travelers met by a stranger on the way to Emmaus: "Were not our hearts burning within us while he was talking to us on the road, while he was opening the scriptures to us?" (Lk. 24:32). Through his writings, as through his teaching and the simple power of his presence, James Dittes has encouraged many of us to take a good look down the road, to see through our expectations to find ministry.

Donald Capps

# Foreword

For the past twenty years I have repeatedly used three of James Dittes' formulations of pastoral wisdom in my teaching and speaking.

Listen to the no's the Dean and I tell our about-to-graduate seminarians in their senior seminar. They are telling you something important about the people's narratives and fears, memories and yearnings, disappointments and sense of mistrust. These no's may even be disclosing something about the nature of human history and biblical faith; certainly they are integral to a cultural and ecclesial context in which the practice of ministry occurs.

Yet we still find that many of our graduates accept their calls with spoken or hidden expectations that they will need to begin by shaping the people up to receive the ministries our students feel they have been prepared to offer. The no's may be responses to the new pastor's desire to purchase a new hymnal, retire the organ and hire a rock band, incorporate inclusive language, or immediately begin to work toward becoming "open and affirming." The people may be deeply entrenched in their opposition to welcoming children to the table (in my own denomination, the United Church of Christ [UCC]) or sending funds to the national office (most mainline denominations). Even worse, they may seem bored or remain silent, not show up, or issue warnings about the dire events that have occurred in former pastorates.

Yet even after our wonderful seminar, they perceive the no's as impediments to one's creative ministry or as yet another mark of a frozen people refusing to be the church. Using a variety of interpretive metaphors and referring to multiple situations, some of our graduates report that the people aren't where "they should be," and they keep insisting on coming before God in their own ways. The no's are to be overcome by better education or preaching, pursuing the denomination's most recent techniques for church growth, or learning how to set up committees so that the yes's might win. It is difficult for them to grasp that no may be a normative response in a broken world, replete with fears of risk, emptiness, and chaos, the presence of strangers, and unprecedented changes. Often pastors cannot even allow the no's at least to attain helpful status as a dimension of assessment.

At other places—and perhaps most effectively with laypersons—I share the metaphor of religion (and religious leadership) as

3

choreographer of the human dance between fundamental needs for autonomy and dependence and the importance of continually negotiating the tensions of competing needs to tighten and loosen bonds in the struggles toward human freedom. This is perhaps most clearly seen in the adolescent, with struggles toward identity marked by rapid shifts between rebellion and compliance, a radical insistence that one doesn't need to be told anything and an often unspoken gesture suggesting that comfort, nurture, and belonging are also fundamental priorities.

But gender dialogue expresses this as well. Expectations that men should be up, invariably up, conflict with longings to receive, to surrender. For the pastor, issues of self-care (even of a spiritual nature) face time demands of always being "for others," to keep busy, to avoid emptiness. Woman pastors refuse to carry the cultural burden of self-sacrifice as if it belonged to one gender and are continually torn between "my or our agenda" (feminism, gay rights, inclusion of strangers) and the needs or readiness of the "others." Dittes' dynamic understandings read even here a yearning for wholeness, and a pastoral eye that can see the inclusive nature of human brokenness and the depths lying behind the human texts that are struggling toward faithfulness in a variety of wildernesses. In Dittes, one finds attention to the partial or masked yes's, which are so disappointing to pastors, and the silent or vehement no's, the normal ways that ordinary folk state human desires and yearnings in the ever-undulating worlds of human history in which churches seek ministry amidst what Rebecca Chopp so eloquently describes as "pulsating temporality."

The third place where I have intentionally incorporated Dittes' wisdom is in conversations and ministries within feminism and other liberation perspectives and, more recently, with dialogue concerning definitions and dynamics of family life and parenting. Feminist pastors (male or female) will need to negotiate existence with their congregations, learning how to put "self" and personal needs on hold without doing damage to their own "self" and integrity. The gay/lesbian pastor shares a world with straight folk. The ordering of his or her personal and political agendas is a matter of complex discernment, not instant announcement. Who am I to be now—and with you? What, after all, is the agenda, or, better yet, *the hope* for ministry?

Few texts in pastoral care refer to the care that must be invested in ecumenical-interfaith dialogue, and Dittes does not address this directly. To remain in fellowship within ecumenical circles, I, as an ordained woman in the United Church of Christ, have to both "let go" my expectations for a church defined by my understanding of polity (without devaluing it) and receive others whose points of view I might have spent years trying to eliminate from my framework of meaning. As an ordained woman, I fellowship with Roman Catholics and the Orthodox and continue to seek dialogue with Missouri Synod Lutherans. Where—and how—do I practice "self-abandonment" and "go out on a limb for God?" Current literature on family and parenting certainly suggests that parenting is a time when self-giving and self-sacrifice are crucial—by both parents—for the nurturing and well-being not only of children but of culture itself. But it is only a time, and there are other times. Dittes' perspectives offer both insight and challenge for us to reflect on these tensions of self-abandonment and self-affirmation, of claiming and letting go, of vulnerability and strength, of care of self and of others.

My intent in writing this foreword is to draw to the attention of a broader audience and, in many ways, a new audience, consideration of these—and many other—wisdoms. The Dittes corpus has not regularly appeared on pastoral care and pastoral theology syllabi, and his writings have been misunderstood by some women pastors and feminist professors of pastoral care, if not written only for men, as having limited applicability for all pastors and pastoral persons. *Au contraire!* My continuing reflections on the practice of ministry and intensive work with students and pastors in a variety of ecclesial contexts and personal embodiments leads me to view the issues of receiving no's, ministry in between competing dynamics and voices (including one's own), and the complex tensions between self-claiming and self-giving (or even of self-abandonment) to be central to the student body that (even as I write this) is preparing to enter Eden Theological Seminary. With what understandings of formation processes and ministerial functions are we inviting them to take on ministry in this complex church and culture? Dittes offers some hard truths to all who dare enter here.

The intention of the title of these essays, *Re-Calling Ministry*, is not to look back, but to summon anew. Through pondering these essays, you are invited to ponder anew issues of formation for ministry, what should be presented in education in the pastoral functions, and what, after all, is the theological context for church and ministry?

According to Dittes, ministry occurs in a broken world, with this fundamental brokenness masked by refusals and resistances, and its apparent emptiness filled up with techniques of restoration (the pastoral functions) that seek to make things right, to shape up a people. In this broken world, cultural expectations that expect men to be up, invariably up, lead to further masks and frustrated yearnings that have had negative effects upon male pastors—and ministry itself. Pastors miss their own data that ministry is hardscrabble and wrought out, not neatly given. There are few more stark statements of ministry as an "impossible possibility" than Dittes', and no clearer statements of the human situation as unambiguous predicament and not a problem or even a series of problems to be solved. For our students nurtured on denominational expectations of church growth in a Willow Creek model, this is hard stuff indeed, because a brokenness that is fundamental and not accidental does not yield to the best of educational processes and growth techniques.

But it is an impossible *possibility*! Help is *in* the wilderness—at the breaking point—where God (as God has always done and will always do) enters the brokenness. God is present precisely at the particular points and places of brokenness. For Dittes is also clear that ministry is both placed and particular; the pastor is destined to experience a fundamental misplacedness and to desire other quarters rather than to reside in the particular place where the people continue to present themselves before God as they choose to do. The God that Dittes portrays here enters the groaning of the folk and finds there the yearnings for wholeness of the human spirit that lie behind the masks and beneath the resistances—but can only be touched by going through, not by skipping over. And this leads to pastoral formation.

The complex processes of pastoral formation must be about more than academic knowledge, functional techniques, and psychological health. The pastor must be able to grieve the people's fundamental inability to respond and the fundamental disappointments where one expected to find exciting yes's and eager partners in the cocreation of new ministerial practices. Along with that, the formation must pay attention to the dynamics of self-abandonment and the kinds of freedom of risking wilderness and chaos in going out on a limb for God—not even by standing on principle but by yielding to historical process. The pastor must be free to make space—to be present at the edges of technical competence. A dimension of this abandonment is to give up habituated responses in order that the people, too, may not only yield their habits but may yield to the wilderness and find new paths. Dittes' reflections upon pastoral situations again and again reveal the habituated response of people meeting the habituated response of pastor leading nowhere—where both refuse the wilderness experience and the fundamental brokenness of a world that the latest techniques cannot patch together. And in the meantime, it can be forgotten that each moment invites depths, as, indeed, the gospel stories that Dittes retells so richly disclose.

So the "impossible possibility" requires pastors capable of full self-investment *and* full abandonment, who find "the stumbling crunchy rhythms" of ministry that each context offers. Knowing that the future will be just as messy, nevertheless the pastor hangs in there with his or her own and the people's faithlessness, waiting for the deepest yearnings to find expression. Without this, instead of the boiling vitality of God, the male minister becomes frozen and limp. Dittes seems to feel that women are better prepared for such a church in such a world. Here he is more hopeful than I, for we may need continually to seek our own erectness, to stand tall for principles or to force "liberation." Both men and women (gay, straight, ethnic) are continually subject to taking on the roles that the people put upon us. At heart, these essays are about pastoral freedom, its dynamics, and varying bondages.

What knowledge functions, then, for those places? Whether in ministries of education, preaching, or administration, the refusals are also data, the no's carry wisdom, and the opportunities for ministry exist in every moment, even those where the people cannot be what the pastor expects, deserves, or desires. The knowledges/techniques of the functions are not primarily to get the folk to where ministry is possible—certainly a lonely practice—but to become viewed as the habituated ways of practice that carry professional value. There is probably no situation that better illustrates this than the UCC trying to use the Willow Creek model to establish new churches. The cultural/sociological analyses are proper, and the techniques are teachable—one does them and the church grows. But whether it does or doesn't, a broken world remains the church's home.

In the final analysis, then, Dittes does not belong in congregational studies or evangelism and church growth. Actually Dittes does not neatly fit anywhere, probably never has, probably never will. This is one of the strengths of these essays; his own yearnings and groaning are visible here. I also have never quite fit in. The amazing claims of these essays are about not fitting in. It is significant that two of his favorite metaphors are of Joseph and the ploughman, hidden, drudging away, keeping their eyes on ordinary tasks, which are really about fields that are fruitful and sons that enter into brokenness. These essays speak to a broken world community where, even in celebration of the new, come the new no's of the new participants. Ecumenical discourse is about unmasking yes's and standing together through no's—discerning the deeper yearnings for the wholeness of a people. I invite you to consider your own ministry through the "being nonbeing" eyes of one who finds healing and hope in misplacedness and broken places.

Peggy A. Way

# Prologue

I think of ministry as the art of making space for others to grow. That seems an apt metaphor for ministry in the name of one who so relentlessly creates and recreates supporting life around us, whose own self-revelation leaves healthy enigma, who, as the supreme act of salvation, "emptied himself…humbled himself and became obedient to the point of death, even death on a cross" (Phil. 2:7–8). Ministry often requires a radical move, requires becoming a vacuum that enables others to loom large. Ministry is the constant sharpening and shaping of questions, more than the giving of answers. Ministry is the giving up of authority and status and acclaim in ways that help others to discover their own authority and status and claims. Ministry is in moving beyond the assumption of roles—recognized, defined patterns and guidelines, agendas for popularity, and checklists for accomplishment—into raw encounters with people at their growing edges, where there is chaos before there is form. Ministry is in renouncing self and in renouncing all the structures that define ministry, because the structures ultimately falsify and impede ministry. Ministry is in going, radically, to the people as they are, rather than insisting that the people come to the minister.

It seems to be the case that women more often and more comfortably practice the ministry of making space, leaving space, for others to move into and grow, while men as ministers more often and more comfortably make space in others' lives a space to be penetrated. So in all professions.

Why is this so? The difference in sexual roles—making space to receive, and making space to penetrate—is a deliberate metaphor, but it is only a metaphor.

Women's openness and "servanthood" might be attributed to a socially imposed passivity. But socially required meekness is, of course, quite different from the voluntary choice of yielding space and power. There is no saving, there is no art, there is no ministry in enforced docility, no more health in anxiety about feeling "up" than in male anxiety for not feeling "up." When women are denied power, they are quite right to claim vigorously the right to power, the option to do with it what they will, including the option to relinquish it in favor of the empowerment of others, an act and art of ministry.

9

Women are freed to pursue space-making ministry, I believe, because they are less harnessed into performance, solo performance, less required to be up. All the ways of eroding others' selfhood, whether by coaching or by targeting or by crippling, are the patterns that men lapse into or are driven into by the relentless pressures to perform and to perform well, pressures that are imposed upon us and that we impose upon ourselves and then impose on all within range. A man can never be up enough to satisfy these demanding voices. One living with this lifelong low-grade anxiety, constantly falling short, constantly falling down, can only envy those who have not been coached into the demands to be up, unfailingly up.

# PART ONE

---

**predicament**, n. a condition, or situation, especially one that is dangerous, unpleasant, embarassing, or, sometimes, comical. Implies a complicated, perplexing situation from which it is difficult to disentangle oneself.

# The Predicament
# of Ministry

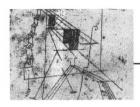

# Ministry as Grief Work

*He was despised and rejected by others;*
*a man of suffering and acquainted with grief...*
*All we like sheep have gone astray;*
*we have all turned to our own way,*
*and the LORD has laid on him the iniquity of us all.*

Isaiah 53:3, 6 (RSV)

To be a minister is to know the most searing grief and abandonment, daily and profoundly. To be a minister is to take as partners in solemn covenant those who are sure to renege. To be a minister is to commit, unavoidably, energy and passion, self and soul, to a people, to a vision of who they are born to be, to their readiness to share and live into that vision. To be a minister is to make that all-out, prodigal commitment to a people who cannot possibly sustain it. That is the nature of ministry, as it is of the God thus served. The minister is called by their need, by their fundamental inability to be who they are born to be, hence by their fundamental inability to share and live into that vision in which the minister invests all. To be a minister, then, as God knows, is to be forsaken regularly and utterly, by those on whose partnership one most relies for identity, meaning, and selfhood, as these are lodged in the vocational commitment. In their forsaking ways the minister's call is rebuffed and repudiated and grieved for over and over again; in their forsaking and in that grief the minister's call is renewed over and over again. For the minister is called by their need, by their fundamental inability to live into the vision and the compact into which the minister must live so totally. Ministry is called forth and occasioned by just such grief. That makes the grief no less painful and no more welcome, only to be recognized.

"How can I be a minister" (which, for ministers, usually means "How can I be anybody?") "if they will not be a church?" are the sorrowful and angry words of grief. But these very words of grieving for ministry are the words that constitute ministry. If they *were* a "church," if they could be the people of God, there would be no need for ministry; there could be no ministry. "I am a minister precisely because they cannot be a church" is the confession of one who recognizes ministry as grief work. The grief is never welcomed or enjoyed, certainly not sought, as though it constituted or certified ministry. But when the grief comes, as it does daily and decisively, it is accepted, and the grief work it occasions is welcomed as ministry. The minister, quite literally, *works through* the grief. Ministry must be in partnership; still more essentially, however, ministry is found in apartness, the apartness of people from themselves; from God; from each other; and, inevitably, from the minister and the ministry they have invited. Facing and sharing that grief, and the grief work it occasions, minister and people can discover a new and more binding kind of partnership, a partnership of apartness.

Other people may experience only a few times in a long lifetime the grief of losing a crucial life partner; the grief of a crucial promise broken by a parent (or a teacher) absolutely trusted until then; the grief of being jilted by a lover, divorced by a spouse, betrayed by a friend. In any one week a minister experiences many such moments of grief. The minister is seduced by the commitments of ministry to put near-ultimate reliance on a partnership, a mutuality, a reciprocity, or a covenant, only to discover daily and painfully that the commitment, so earnest on one side, is one-sided.

To be a minister is to be like a ballet dancer straining all muscles and energies into a daring leap only to find the partner not there to make the catch or steady the landing. To be a minister is to have learned one's role in a play well, to be committed to the message of the play and passionately geared for a performance, and to appear on stage to discover the rest of the cast in disarray, unprepared, or absent. To be a minister is like being married to someone who is not married to you.

Most other professionals hold back some selfhood to invest in family, hobbies, luncheon clubs, days off, or even church. A minister is all-out a minister, and usually nothing but a minister, twenty-four hours a day. So when ministry is thwarted and the minister feels not a minister, there is the emptiness and grief of being nobody. Most other professionals find their "clients" dependent on them; clients follow the rules and roles set by the lawyer, nurse, auto mechanic, or physician. But ministers are in a partnership. Their work depends on invitation and response from others. Lawyers and physicians and nurses and auto mechanics take charge. Ministers plant seeds.

Moreover, ministers plant seeds—on purpose, as part of their ministry—on rocky soil, where the seeds are mostly doomed. Where the soil is good and the climate is nourishing, there is no need for ministry; plants seed themselves naturally and grow abundantly. Some ministers do seek haven from grief, and hence from ministry, where faith and community, perhaps even love and justice, do seem to be thriving abundantly. But the ministry of the God who has ever pursued an apostate people precisely in their faithlessness and brokenness is called to flourish exactly where it can never flourish, in those corners of life where it is most needed and hence most unwelcome. When the minister hears a comfortable affirmation and acceptance, there may be cause for self-scrutiny. Ministry may still lie ahead. When the people say no, ministry may have been reached. Ships are meant to travel through the waves of the high seas; if the surface is always placid, they must still be in the harbor.

## "Acquainted with Grief..."

To grieve is to take two coffee cups from the cupboard in the morning, only to remember that one's wife is dead or separated...and to have to put one cup back.

To grieve is to start joyfully into the gift shop, one's eye attracted by the perfect gift in the window, only to remember that the child is dead...and to walk on down the street, heavily.

To grieve is to start out from the office with habitual joy at the end of the day, toward the usual rendezvous with one's lover, only to remember the long, anguished phone call of the night before...and to go home alone.

To grieve is to be delighted with the snapshot prints at the drugstore counter and impulsively to order duplicates to share with one's mother, only to remember that she died six months previously...and to say to the clerk, "Never mind."

To grieve is to have an especially interesting job come into the shop, a job one automatically routes to a favorite young protege, only to have the word come back that he has just quit and gone to work for a competitor...and to look up, confused, saying, "Who can do this?"

To grieve is to wake up on a brilliant sunny morning with spontaneous, unbidden anticipation of playing golf, only to be reminded instantly by heavy limbs that one has had a stroke...and to close one's eyes, now moist.

To grieve is to invest prime energy and love into a sermon for a much-loved people, only to be reminded that it was not heard: "I enjoyed your sermon." "That was a cute illustration." "Wasn't the choir lovely this morning?"

To grieve is to pour one's energies for months and years into the struggles of a beleaguered minority group or a beleaguered marriage or a beleaguered teenager—standing by patiently and wisely and lovingly, and indeed making a crucial difference—only to have the group or couple or teenager, having found themselves, shun you as a threatening enemy.

To grieve is to introduce into a discussion at the deacons' meeting some biblical allusions, such as some of the ringing phrases from Romans 8, as one has spent years training oneself to do and supposes to be standard in a Christian community, only to have the deacons look blankly at you and someone remark, "You ministers sometimes do pick up some funny language."

To grieve is to presuppose among one's people a Christian concern for the oppressed and to build upon this foundation an alertness to the problem of civil rights for homosexuals or Puerto Ricans, only to have this foundation manifestly absent: "Stick to religion and to our own kind of people."

To grieve is to commit oneself seriously to the pulpit committee's assurance that the people of the church want to develop intentional small groups, such as house churches and prayer cells, only to discover the utmost resistance: "Well, folks are pretty busy here in the evenings; Sunday morning is about all we can manage."

To grieve is to accept the pulpit committee's assurance that the people would not be prejudiced against a woman as minister and that she could function effectively, only to be confronted by a barrage of offensive putdowns.

To grieve is to have one's earnest readiness to share the depths of the people's lives frustrated repeatedly by their attempt to assign one to superficial roles: "Just give the invocation at the women's luncheon; please try to get around to each of our homes at least once a year, even though you can't stay long."

To grieve is to prepare earnestly for the training session that the church school teachers asked for, only to have them spend the entire evening preoccupied with discipline problems for the individual students, problems about getting supplies in and out of the supply closet, and questions of scheduling the year-end picnic.

To grieve is to invest years of heady anticipation and hearty preparation in taking one's place as the minister among the people of God, only to discover the visions of that anticipation and the fruits of that preparation disparaged and frustrated by those very people. The visions have been bolstered by so much: by the study of church history, disclosing the high unassailed and unambiguous status of clergy in the established churches of the past; by memories of one's childhood and adolescence when total loving support seemed to close around the minister or oneself as the "pretheolog"; by the offhand abstract language of much transcendental theology so deliberately out of touch with the realities of the institutional church as to speak easily and glibly of the committed people of God, or the functioning body of Christ as though it were fact; by most teaching of pastoral theology, which instructs a minister how to take a part in the script by assuming all the others are playing their parts; by one's own lifelong yearnings for a closely supporting community; by the rhetoric of ordination sermons.

The vision is also sustained by the very impediments in the preparation for ministry. Sterile seminars in Bible and theology, if endured, seem justified by that vision of the community soon to be entered in which Bible and theology are validated and learned by being lived. The belittling tendered the apprentice theological student by a training church enhances the vision of the time one will assume a full and respected place as the minister.

Through theological training and into first assignments one can endure many years of anguish and ambiguity by keeping this lofty vision. One can be sustained and guided through an entire ministry by the vision, so long as it is kept apart and beyond, never located, never confused with a particular people or place or program. Knowing full well that no community, no parish, no people can embody the vision—through such grief work, anticipating the death of the vision by knowing it cannot fully live, the minister stays in ministry.

To locate the vision, to ground it in a place and people, to try to lodge it in a program or parish who cannot but dislodge it, sooner or later—that is to invite grief without preparing for it. When the vision is identified with a particular assignment or community—one's first full-time church, one's first church as the senior minister, those people in the inner city who are committed and free of the shackles of the institutional church, or the church in the university town where people are literate about Bible and theology—or with particular people—the counselee with whom one has developed such close rapport through long, intimate hours, the one family who seems on the same wavelength with each other and with you, the no-nonsense group of businessmen working with you on the public housing project—such grounding of vision sets one up for grief. For no people, no person can ever become that fully responsible, fully responsive partner to ministry envisioned by theological abstraction, personal yearning, or historical simplification. Yet ministry nevertheless seems to require and propel that intensity of investment, that dancer's leap, that actor's total immersion into a role that presupposes just such unswerving partners, invested and totally committed.

# Swallowing Grief

*He was oppressed, and he was afflicted,*
*yet he did not open his mouth;*
*like a lamb that is led to the slaughter,*
*and like a sheep that before its shearers is silent,*
*so he did not open his mouth.*

Isaiah 53:7

There are two ways to swallow grief dumbly, both ways making it more poisonous than nutritious. One can deny the life that was lived, the partnership that was shared. Or one can deny the death, the real limits and breakdown of the partnership. The widower can throw away the now-offending second coffee cup and the jilted lover can burn the letters, as though the life and love had never been lived and shared. Death is triumphant. Or the widower can continue to make the second cup of coffee, keep all of his wife's clothes and room as they were, and the lover can continue to haunt the rendezvous and reread the letters as though they were fresh, just as though nothing had changed, just as though the partnership persisted, undaunted. Death is denied.

The minister can swallow grief either way: death triumphant or death denied. The minister can repudiate the visions, deny the tremendous and total investment made in them, exaggerate the abandonment by partners, see only the assault on the vision, not the visions. That is, the minister can flee the ministry, either by actually resigning from the church payroll or by becoming resigned to a visionless, partnerless occupation, by becoming jaded and "professional," mechanically going through the motions, like a zombie actor reciting long-memorized lines on a darkened and empty stage to an empty house. This is the path some take, stockading themselves, darkening the house, with drink, with golf, with cynical banter with fellow professionals. These are the ministers that novelist John Updike knows and portrays so well. They have protected their visions by abandoning them and by no longer caring whether they have partners or effect. They go through the motions. The motions may be those of worship or preaching or counseling or municipal politics or jovial backslapping or studying or more efficient administrative operations or personal spirituality. But, like the jilted lover who hides from further grief by staying home evenings and reading romantic stories, such ministry-like motions are totally self-contained and get nowhere. The minister, purposely defensive, heeds not the needs or reactions of prospective partners. The minister hears only the no.

Or the minister may cling tenaciously to the vision and expectation of partnership and deny its limits, which are clearly evident in the practice of ministry. The minister pretends not to hear the no. The minister may find or seek out those few—celebrated as "the faithful remnant"—who seem to offer the maximum possibility of partnership and concentrate ministry on them, who least need it. Or the minister may find a few selective avenues of ministry that seem to generate a response—counseling often seems to make people warm and responsive, political action puts one in touch with those who know how to stroke back. And effective ministry will be stockaded as safely as possible, like the jilted lover closeted and reading old love letters.

The death-defying minister's intense addiction to a few forms may not be much different from the jaded minister's casualness about going through the motions. Both protect themselves from facing the grief of disappointment in partnership, past and future, by effectively shielding themselves with the motions of ministry from the majority of those to whom they would minister but from whom they feel separated by the risk of broken covenant.

There is a common way of denying the seriousness of the no, of clinging to the expectations of partnership and denying the radical violation of the partnership that does in fact exist. This is to suppose that the people's "delinquencies" need just a bit more coaching and training to remedy. The people's failing in partnership is not taken *seriously*; it is seen as only a temporary and technical defect. They can be taught from the pulpit or from the Bible or from the denominational manuals, from the longings of the minister's heart and from the abstractions of theology. Having been taught the script, they will, it is assumed, readily play the part. Let the people be scolded or instructed or cajoled into proper partnership. The minister's vision is grounded just on the other side of this locker room pep talk: In the second half of this ministry, the team will be functioning smoothly.

Another way of trivializing the failure of partnership takes the form of the occasional journalistic account of distress in a particular church where conflict or dissonance between minister's expectations and people's expectations have surfaced, as though this is news, an unusual event. Or the minister may simply swallow the grief quite literally, keep it private, personal, and ignored. He or she will go relentlessly on, oblivious to the disappointments of failed partnership, heedless of the dance leaps taken and uncaught, the supporting cast in disarray. This is a heroic posture of ministry and perhaps a necessary one. But it, like the other responses, swallows the grief, refuses to take seriously the visions and their frustration, and so fails to learn from the grief and to find ministry *in* the grief.

## Working through Grief

*Yet it was the will of the LORD to bruise him;*
*he has put him to grief...*
*the will of the LORD shall prosper in his hand;*
*he shall see the fruit of the travail of his soul and be satisfied;*
*by his knowledge shall the righteous one, my servant,*
*make many to be accounted righteous.*

Isaiah 53:10–11 (RSV)

22

It is the extraordinary claim of Christian and Jewish faith that God works through grief. Contradicting all natural expectations (and especially the American prizing) of the efficacy of smoothness and disclosing, in the midst of brokenness and in desolation of spirit—indeed out of the very raw materials of brokenness and desolation—come a wholeness more substantial and a life more vital than can be found otherwise. From creation out of chaos to the promise of salvation in the midst of apocalypse, the Bible records the works of a God who fashioned a people out of slaves, wanderers, and exiles; an intimate and lasting covenant out of the most faithlessly broken covenant; dramatic life out of the most forsaken death; a community of faith out of those in most fearful disarray.

The record of the Old Testament is nothing if not the record of a God who experiences the constant grief of the abandonment of his people, and who enters into that abandonment and lives into that grief to unlock the creative energies within it. It is only after Adam and Eve have violated their first covenant and are hiding in fear and shame that God seeks them out, first appears to them face to face, and sets in motion a drama of salvation that takes with utmost seriousness the persisting bond between God and people and with equal seriousness the ruptures to that bond. It is in the squalid faithlessness of the Jewish people, time after time after time abandoning their part of the partnership with God, that God is most powerfully present, scourging the rupture to the bond with fierce wrath, tenderly nurturing the remnant of bond that is within the very experience of grief. Indeed, the Lord of the Old Testament knows precisely what it is to "see the fruit of the travail of his soul and be satisfied."

The record of the New Testament is nothing if not precisely the story of ministry in the midst of broken expectations as in no other place; indeed, the story of a message and a ministry conveyed *by means of* broken expectations. Incarnate deity in a village stable confounded the wisest expectations of the wise men. (But by taking seriously both the commitment in those expectations and their radical destruction, they learned a lesson.) Jesus' ministry consistently frustrated the highest religious expectations of the Jewish people as recorded in their law and guarded by the lawkeepers. Jesus' ministry with his disciples was one disappointment after another, as each repeatedly frustrated the expectations of the other. Jesus would not dispute and teach as a good rabbi should but rather indirectly, in parables and in deeds. The cheering Palm Sunday crowd abandoned him, as he abandoned their expectations. He celebrated communion in the midst of betrayal and finally lived out salvation in the most forlorn of deaths. The teaching and the work of Christ proceeded precisely by means of breaking expectations. Jesus caused grief, and Jesus suffered grief; the grief was necessary for the uncovering of wholeness. If people had persisted in living only in their expectations, they would have kept themselves separated from God— the fate of the Pharisees; so, too, with those who abandoned their expectations, once frustrated, such as the rich young ruler. Wise men, disciples, women, finally Jesus himself, in the agony of Gethsemane and Golgotha, persisted in living *in* their grief and abandonment and wresting from it new vision, new commitment, new guidance, and new personhood. It is the *intent* of the Lord to reach people in grief, his and theirs, as perhaps they can be reached in no other way. "It was the will of the LORD to bruise him; he has put him to grief..."

The creative healing power of grief is dramatically confirmed in human experience—so long as one is dealing with real grief, which denies neither the dreams nor their dashing, denies neither the commitment nor its betrayal, denies neither the expectations nor their frustrations, denies neither life nor death—so long as one takes seriously, in the grief, the earnestness of the vision and the earnestness of its shattering.

23

Lovers disappoint each other bitterly, yet, holding fast to the radical commitment that has made them so vulnerable to the disappointments and taking equally seriously the severity of the disappointment and the grief, they enfold each other and find in their mingled tears and despair an intimacy and a trust and a hope far greater than that which they found dashed.

The new widower takes down two coffee cups and then sadly puts one back; there is both a shared life to be celebrated and a death to be recognized; in the grief he ponders in such moments, in that quick review of his life with, and now without, his wife, he comes to enhanced and deepened appreciation of the relationship and of himself in separation from her. He is more a whole person and readier to enter new relationships for having lived through such moments of grief.

The young woman is in despair as she recovers from her hysterectomy. She does not deny the loss and the grief by clinging blindly to the now-impossible dream of having children, nor does she deny the grief by repudiating that vision with a callous shrug. Instead, she lives into that grief by living into the vision and into its defeat until she discovers deeper aspirations and fulfillments. The personal fulfillment, indeed the experience of motherhood, is not to be denied even though giving birth is to be denied. Her spirit is opened to new vocational possibilities, new forms of motherhood, once she faces fully her grief and sees in it two things: the deep aspirations that were lodged in her hopes for children and frustrated by the hysterectomy; and the absoluteness of that frustration, the complete death of her hopes for children of her own. Facing her grief means facing the depth of her hopes and the depths of her despair; facing her grief becomes the means of finding new expression for those hopes.

The call to the ministry functions in the same way. There is a call to the covenants of ministry, then constant frustration of the expectation built into that call, then formidable and powerful re-call to ministry in the grief of those frustrations. This seems not unlike the redemptive processes displayed in the Bible and the intentions of God as recorded in Isaiah: "Yet it was the will of the LORD to bruise him; he has put him to grief...the will of the LORD shall prosper in his hand; he shall see the fruit of the travail of his soul and be satisfied" (RSV). The minister is called into a ministry of grief, is re-called to deepen and reform and refresh and redirect that ministry by, quite literally, working through the grief that befalls every venture into ministry. The minister is re-called to ministry by working through the grief of failed partnerships, the grief experienced by the minister in the abandonment of those to whom ministry is directed and with whom it is to be shared. "How can I be a minister when they will not be a church?" This is not a hopeless question. But the answer comes through facing, not denying, the grief that it presupposes.

The minister is called to particular partnerships, to particular roles that require others to play corresponding and reciprocal roles. Indeed, ministry of the living God who works in history and by incarnation does not exist if it is not lodged or placed in particular callings, in specific covenants and partnerships with particular people at particular times and places. The call to ministry often comes precisely in such callings, personal needs to be met, organizational rhythms and systems with a place to be filled, traditions to be lived out. Yet such callings, in particular times and places by particular people, can never make good the call they make. We must not ignore the disappointments and abandonments—inevitable and healthy—with which ministers' partners must eventually respond to ministry. These abandonments, if the grief is lived into, themselves become new callings. (We must not deny the abandonment and frustration that ministers supply their partners. Ministers, too, let down the partnership. I do not deny this, but neither is this my present concern. Others scold ministers for their delinquencies. I attempt here to support them in their distress and to redirect the energies of despair.)

Preaching, teaching, counseling, enabling deacons, arranging committees, leading prayer, pricking consciences, organizing picketing or petitions—all respond to a bidding, a calling by another person, a need or readiness expressed implicitly or explicitly, and presuppose a response in partnership. The minister moves and expects a reciprocal move by the people. Sometimes that happens; the dancers are in step, the ecological system is in balance. Frequently it does not happen; the dancers are out of step, a disruptive mutation dislodges the partnership out of its ecological niche. The people fail to make the complementary move. (The people say no, the people fail to say thank you, the people get distracted and preoccupied with organizational machinery.) Or the people make another move, an unexpected move, which seems to call from the minister a move that contradicts ministry. (The people say pray, the people say heal, the people say perform, the people say sacrifice.) The momentum of ministry is stopped, the call contradicted, the partnership betrayed. There is reason for all of the grief the minister feels and more. What *is* necessary is that the minister experience the grief fully, live fully in it, work fully through it; repudiate neither the authenticity and loftiness of the call to which ministry was responding, the importance of the partnership that was expected, nor deny the genuineness and fullness and authenticity of the betrayal, the frustration. The people *did* say no after they said yes and after the minister was lured by the yes. Fully viewed, taking both the yes and the no absolutely seriously, the grief transforms the partnership and re-calls to ministry; it does not end the partnership of ministry.

## Taking the Yes Seriously

The people meant their calling and whatever the calling meant to them. From their perspective, their present no is in continuity with the earlier yes. Jesus said he came to fulfill the law, not to repudiate it, even as he systematically frustrated all those expectations of people based on the law. The law affirmed something Jesus wanted to affirm, pointed to something Jesus wanted to point to. If one can believe the yes and not fear to look for it in the no, one will find it. The no is a word in the conversation and has a meaning in the conversation. It does not end the conversation.

If the people say, "We enjoyed your sermon," perhaps they do not mean to slight it or to put it aside; perhaps that is only their way—their only way—of talking about it. Perhaps they mean simply: "We were touched or moved or pricked by the sermon, too much so to verbalize it comfortably; so we both express and disguise this reaction with 'enjoyed your sermon.'" Perhaps they mean: "We admire your learning and wisdom, your knowledge of the Bible, and your ability to make it speak to us, so much that we are intimidated and do not know how to enter into your league." Perhaps they mean: "You made us angry, but we never felt permission to be angry in church." And perhaps the response means just what the minister likely feels it means: a stuporous, bland, heedless, perhaps even inattentive, reception. But what does *this* mean among the churchgoers? Why do people persistently come to church and persistently not hear? This is still part of some awestruck wonder at the word. If people do feel themselves unworthy or unneedy, if the spoken word is too lofty or too mean or too mysterious and arcane, why do they come? Or if they come, why do they persistently turn off? There is *some* dialogue going on. The people *are* responding, if the minister has ears to hear. Just as the first invitation to preach the sermon or their attendance at the worship service are a placing of their lives into some kind of relationship with the word as preached, so is their response at the end of the sermon. Though their response may not be what the minister expected in the partnership, the minister would do well to assume that the people are still in the partnership. Their response transforms the covenant and the call by extending it.

If the minister listens to the no for what it means strictly in the short run to him or her, the minister, then there is heard only the denial of expectations. But the minister can listen to the response for what it means to the people and hence to the minister and ministry in the long run.

There is a literalistic reading of people that is sometimes practiced even by ministers who have become quite sophisticated about reading the Bible without literalistic shackles. Such literalism skims off, at face value, the superficial level of people's response. Because the minister reads glibly, he or she easily assumes that the people are being glib, that the no means quite literally only what it seems to mean at first hearing. The more sophisticated minister reads the words of the Bible in the context in which they were written and asks what they meant to the writer before asking what they may mean to the reader. What spoken or unspoken implications, what cultural or individualized connotations of the language are there for the speaker? In that particular context, what impact, larger than any literal reading of the words, did the speaker or writer mean to communicate? Why not accord contemporary church people the same sophistication of intention, either conscious or unconscious, and learn to read their words for what they mean to *them* in *their* context?

## Taking the No Seriously

Much as the people's response is part of the continuing partnership, it is a rebuff to the minister's move, and intended to be so. The minister has responded to the call, but apparently not quite on target. The minister has entered into the compact, but with too compacted a ministry, has fit into too narrow an ecological niche. The people seem to be saying, "We feel you, but not exactly where we hurt or yearn; we are not there." The minister's role is going to have to be transformed.

This asks for a sacrifice by the minister. Not the simple sacrifice of high salary or high social status; those things are given up relatively easily. The sacrifice is being willing to lose one's identity, to be swallowed up into chaos. For the minister does make the moves of sermon or any other role of ministry with an energy and an investment and an ultimacy in which they provide identity and important meaning to the minister. This is why the minister is so ready to hear the resistive response as an attack; there is much of importance here to be defensive about. The minister is asked to respond to the experience of taking a flying leap and finding no one there to steady the landing by taking another flying leap in a different direction in a style for which there has been no practice or script and to a place where again there may be no partner.

Remember that the people's words do *not* provide close literal guidance for the new calling. They are only saying: "We are not just where you are aiming." To take literally their call to pray or heal or anything else is surely to enter into a new blind alley. One needs to probe beneath the surface of their calling to find the new call within it. Sometimes this probing can be done verbally, until the minister does feel some assurance about the new target and the new response, hears the new call. But sometimes a minister has to probe behaviorally, not verbally, beneath the resistive response that is a re-calling. The minister has to take the leap, has to venture a new response and see where it gets.

Indeed, most ministry is probably in this chaotic, interim mode. Seldom in stable balance, the ecology is more often in a state of disruption, which means it is always evolving. Most of us live by the light-at-the-end-of-the-tunnel myth that points to a time when all *will* be stable, and one can settle down to ministry with partners responding as expected. In fact, a yes response, an apparently stable partnership, may be the most resistive and denying of all; it may well represent a sophisticated encapsulation of the minister by really shackling ministry, keeping it in a box, keeping it from reaching out effectively into disruption.

Ministry is not in answering questions or in having questions answered. Ministry is precisely in the creative process of continually reshaping questions and reshaping answers. Ministry is in the process of re-calling, reforming, revisioning, ever peeling off what is partial and encrusted in human resignation and contentment with forms in order to leave room for the boiling vitality of God's creative, redemptive spirit.

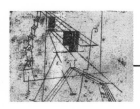

# 2

# Ministry: In Place, No Place

*When the days drew near for him to be taken up, he set his face to go to Jerusalem. And he sent messengers ahead of him. On their way they entered a village of the Samaritans to make ready for him; but they did not receive him, because his face was set toward Jerusalem. When his disciples James and John saw it, they said, "Lord, do you want us to command fire to come down from heaven and consume them?" But he turned and rebuked them. Then they went on to another village.*

*As they were going along the road, someone said to him, "I will follow you wherever you go." And Jesus said to him, "Foxes have holes, and birds of the air have nests; but the Son of Man has nowhere to lay his head." To another he said, "Follow me." But he said, "Lord, first let me go and bury my father." But Jesus said to him, "Let the dead bury their own dead; but as for you, go and proclaim the kingdom of God." Another said, "I will follow you, Lord, but let me first say farewell to those at my home." Jesus said to him, "No one who puts a hand to the plow and looks back is fit for the kingdom of God."*

*After this the Lord appointed seventy others and sent them on ahead of him in pairs to every town and place where he himself intended to go. He said to them…"Carry no purse, no bag, no sandals; and greet no one on the road. Whatever house you enter, first say, 'Peace to this house! And if anyone is there who shares in peace, your peace will rest on that person; but if not, it will return to you. Remain in the same house, eating and drinking whatever they provide, for the laborer deserves to be paid. Do not move about from house to house. Whenever you enter a town and its people welcome you, eat what is set before you; cure the sick who are there, and say to them, 'The kingdom of God has come near to you.' But whenever you enter a town and they do not welcome you, go out into the streets and say, 'Even the dust of your town that clings to our feet, we wipe off in protest against you. Yet know this: the kingdom of God has come near.'"*

Luke 9:51—10:11

## Ministry in Place: Rooted and Routed

Christian ministry must be in a place. The passage of scripture above, which testifies so dramatically to the radical placelessness of Jesus' ministry and of those who would follow him, testifies equally dramatically to the placedness of ministry. Jesus' ministers must leave home and duties and possessions; they may or may not find lodging. But ministry must be lodged, fixed. This passage speaks of Jesus setting his face resolutely toward a place and of his intention to lodge in particular places along the way. God's intention to save the race finds only localized expression, in visits to particular dusty villages. When those on mission find lodging in a house, they are to stay in that house, however mean and confining it may seem, however much more grand and compelling the mission may seem.

To be sure, Jesus' ministry and all ministry in his name must ultimately break out of the structures—and break the structures themselves—in which we contain our lives, for the structures that house and shelter *do* confine and distort. But first, minister and ministry must inhabit those structures, as genuinely and as radically as God has inhabited human history; for the breaking, to be truly liberating, must come from within; blasting of structures from without tends to destroy the inhabitants along with the structures. The cost, of course—as unacceptable as it is necessary— is that ministry that truly lodges in structures consigns itself to suffer their fate and to become broken too.

To become located and lodged in a particular fragment of human history, with a particular people, is the only way, God knows, to enter history redemptively. That is as true for a minister today becoming fully invested in a particular denomination, a particular parish, a particular household, a particular program within that parish, a particular conversation with a particular person—obscure and remote and mean as that parish may be—as it is for God becoming fully incarnate among particular people in a particular locality, as obscure and remote and mean as that setting may have been. But also to become located and lodged in a particular fragment of human history, God knows, is to suffer the constrictions and rupture and grief that are the inevitable consequence of the localization and fragmentation. This is as true for a minister today suffering the grief over the failure or the constrictions of a parish program in which he or she has made a full investment as it is for God absorbing the pain and brokenness of a pained and broken people.

In the midst of the dramatic warnings of the nomadic placelessness and rootlessness of his ministry, Jesus just as dramatically uses a remarkable metaphor of fixedness and focus: the plowman. The fisherman or even the sower are more romantic and therefore more appealing metaphors. They cast nets or seeds, widely, uncertainly, yet hopefully. They expect many empty nests and unsprouted seeds, yet occasional and eventual rich harvests. Venturing wide areas of sea and of turf, and taking a long view of time while they patiently await a high yield, surely fishermen and sowers are metaphors more suited to the ministry of the itinerant Son of man who has no place to lay his head. And elsewhere Jesus does use these metaphors. But just here, while emphasizing placelessness, he also invites his followers to be like the plowman, head down, not looking about, making a narrow rut and being careful to stay in it. Ministry, even the ministry that breaks itself open to new life, even the ministry of those ministers who must recognize themselves as nomadic pilgrims—especially such ministry—must be in place.

Ministers are "placed" in their positions by bishops and synod presidents and by placement services of churches and theological schools. But the more crucial placement is done by the people themselves, as they signal to the minister just what place a minister has in their lives: the moral exemplar, the surrogate holy one, the good mother or father, maybe the pied piper whom the children all like and obey, the healer of marital discord, the salver of all conflict, the answerer of unanswerable questions, the asker of embarrassing questions, the presider over a social status institution, the fragile link with a God once believed in or yearned for, the reminder of a simpler and purer lifestyle once enjoyed or yearned for, the surrogate believer or Bible reader or prayer or good neighbor to those in need—there is an endless number of places a minister occupies in the lives of people. For each person the place is different. For each person the place is usually well established and more or less clearly signaled. Such placement is seldom what the minister would choose.

Early New England churches would ordain a minister only to a particular parish; when the ministry in that parish ended, so did the ordination. The minister was no longer "reverend" until another particular people decided to call him so. Practically speaking, and any high theological convictions about the indelibility of ordination notwithstanding, this is still true. In a new parish a minister still must discover what it means to be "minister" in that place. Even more important, each individual "ordains" a minister every time the person says or thinks "reverend," every time the person tells the minister: Speak in a loud voice as though you had authority. Baptize my baby, and I will come back again when I have my next baby. Bury my father, as you did my grandfather. Come visit our home or our club and bless our food, but don't stay too long. Explain to the deacons where to stand while they are serving communion. Tell my boy to get off drugs. Can you find me a job? What are some good things to see if we visit Israel? Can you fix the mail slot on the church door? Be a man, but not *too* masculine; have an attractive wife who is not too sexy; have well-behaved children who are also well rounded. The daily ordaining calls are meaner and much less welcome than the ordination rhetoric that the minister would prefer. The abodes that Jesus' emissary is welcomed to are far less grand than expected by one sent out to proclaim the kingdom. Yet they are real places where people live and which they invite the minister to inhabit. If the minister is to find a place in their lives, it must be, at least initially, in the place thus reserved. If the minister tries to carve or claim a different place, to say, "I belong in your life here, not there," then the people are as amazed and perturbed as the householder who finds the guest choosing or imagining quarters different from those especially reserved. Then the people say no.

When Jesus entered *his* city, Jerusalem, he found himself welcomed to a place in the people's lives—that of the conquering Messiah, proclaimed with hosannas—for which he knew he was misfit. But he occupied that place, playing the role to the hilt, living out their myths and expectations, because he needed to reach them to occupy their lives as they were lived. To decline the place reserved for him would be to act as though he were unwelcome altogether. The shaking off of the dust is not for those who offer a mean or unfit place, but only for those who offer no place at all.

When ministers are placed, they often feel *mis*placed. When ministers find a place reserved just for them—for *ministers*—in the lives of people, it is not always—in fact, it seldom is—the kind of place they would choose for themselves. Ministers would prefer other quarters than those they are shown to. (Indeed, after they lodge long enough with the people, they almost always *are* offered a different place in their household, usually a place different from that the people first designated and different from that the minister would first have asked for.) Ministers would usually prefer a place closer to the family's intimate life and less "guest"-like. Ministers may prefer hospitality that is more informal, or else more formal, than what they are offered.

When ministers feel misplaced, they often confuse this with feeling unwelcome. When people offer them a place, even insist on a place of their own choosing, ministers may experience this as denying their own preferences (which may be spoken or unspoken, heard or unheard) and hence as a way of saying no to the ministers personally. Ministers feel unwelcome and feel like shaking the dust off with vigor and vehemence.

Exactly the opposite is true. What the minister experiences as misplacement is the strongest possible evidence of hearty welcome, even desperate welcome. The minister is welcomed into the people's lives in a place of their choosing, because that is important to them. The more they insist on showing the minister effusively to the quarters reserved just for "minister," and the more they are deaf to the minister's hints that different lodgings would be preferable, the more certain the minister can be that he or she *is* welcome, is wanted, is needed, really does have a place, a crucial and otherwise empty place, precisely in these reserved quarters. Precisely their deafness to the minister's hints for different lodging is what should make the minister want to listen all the more keenly to the hints as to why *this* lodging is so important for the people. Why do they need a biblical authority, or a question answerer, or a problem solver, so badly that they cannot hear the minister's clear hints of discomfort about being lodged in such places?

Coming into people's lives as a minister is like coming on stage in the late act of a long play, filling a part that has been well established in earlier acts, by different actors, and after a lot of dramatic action that has enmeshed that part with the role of others. No minister starts fresh to create the role to his or her liking (or to the liking of professors or others who have coached the minister in how to play the role). The role is well established in its relations with others. The drama has gone on long enough to structure the plot securely, so that whatever part the minister has now is essential in the economy of the drama. To be sure, the drama is not finished, and the new minister will begin to reshape the story. But the reshaping does not begin afresh; it begins where the drama now is. The minister can begin to learn from the reactions of others just what this role is and maybe even begin to infer its history.

That this minister is not treated as he or she wants to be treated but is treated as the people want—that is the strongest possible evidence of an important and welcome place in their lives.

To be a minister is sometimes like overhearing one side of a telephone conversation but not realizing it is a conversation with a third party. Suppose you are in one room and you hear a person in another room speaking. The words sound strange, a bit off focus, not really directed to you as you understand yourself. "I wish you wouldn't play your music so loud," you might hear, when you don't even play music at all. You start to defend yourself, to straighten out the speaker, to explain how wrong he is about you. Then you walk into the speaker's room and discover that he is not talking to you at all; he is on the telephone. Suddenly you can drop your defensiveness, empathize with the speaker, join him in his complaint against the loud music. Being a minister is very much like that—with the special complication that people are often looking right at you instead of talking into the telephone. But what is happening is exactly the same: People only *seem* to be talking to you when, in fact, they are dealing with somebody else, and they need your help to do that. Even though you are in the room where you know you belong, when they place you, they are really talking on the telephone to somebody else, and they need you by their side, in their room, while they do that. To be a minister is to give up your preferred place and to be willing to be misplaced, in order to be in the people's place; then to experience the no-place—or perhaps the new place—of standing by.

## Leaving Place to Find Place

*Let the same mind be in you that was in Christ Jesus, who,*
*though he was in the form of God, did not regard equality with*
*God as something to be exploited, but emptied himself.*
Philippians 2:5–7

To be a minister is to know the theological (and maybe even the sociological and psychological) significance of baptism—and to be right about that and able to communicate it meaningfully—yet still to be willing, for the time being, to give all that up and to accept the misplacement of being called in merely and casually to baptize the new baby. Such misplacement is accepted in order to have *a* place in the life of the parents, the only place they have available for a minister now. Maybe it's like having to be born in a stable because there is no room in the inn, or even like riding a donkey and fitting into people's hosannaed expectations of messiah even when you know better. Once in place though misplaced, then ministry proceeds in the new place, which feels like no place, which is located, and momentarily bounded by, the parents' urgent need to have the baby baptized. Ministry is to stand by in that place, in their place, and give them room to discover more fully whatever yearnings and fears are lodged in their earnest questions, and also to discover whatever responses these yearnings and fears are pointing to. Ministry is to accept the misplacement so as to open it up, address it, and come to find it replaced. The parents' misplacing concerns may be several: awareness that their parents, who expect baptism and many other things, are looking over their shoulders; some sense of presumption and loneliness in daring to have a child and make claims of adulthood; some "Is that all there is?" letdown ambivalently mixed with the joys and hopes of child rearing; some dim sense (more and more likely these days from ecological consciousness than from any explicit Christian theology) that any new life is to be held in precious stewardship and to be shared as a hedge against squandering.

It sometimes happens that parents, exploring these misplacing concerns with sufficient freedom and space, come to address them with just those theological ideas the minister could have announced in the first place. It also sometimes happens that both parents and minister come to new places, the minister replacing his or her initial ideas, too, or at least discovering that they find new focus as they find locus. Ministry that declines the proffered placement as unsuitable seldom finds lodging or effect.

Ministry is *in* all of the displacing demands and denials—just say the table grace at our club dinner, don't speak of homosexuals, live the closely inspected exemplary life, accept the 10 percent discounts and other demeaning courtesies—without ever being defined by them. They locate ministry but do not identify it. They indicate *where* a minister can respond but not how.

## Accommodations Resisted

Ministers wrestle with their calls, even as did those whom Jesus commissioned; they must decide whether to lodge or to move on. There are more formal and public calls: the call to ministry, whether to lodge in one particular vocation or another; and the call to a parish, whether to lodge in one particular location or another. When these public calls are at stake, the minister is expected to and accustomed to struggle, to try to discover whether the welcome (and needs and possibilities) of that "village" outweigh its limitations, chiefly the limitation that it is only *a* village, one of many. Ministers recognize that they must give up some of their own preconceived or preferred expectations as to ideal vocation or ideal location, and also abandon, or learn to live with, misgivings about the proffered call. Jesus told his followers to test out the village. Ministers know how to test out the village when they are dealing with these more formal and public calls.

The informal daily, even hourly, calls that are lodged in particular conversations with particular people are just as crucial, just as fraught with the same questions, just as much in need of struggle and testing; yet it is not expected or even accepted that ministers should respond to these calls with the same testing, the same deliberate abandon or expectations, the same deliberate immersion into what is recognized as only a lodging—only *a* lodging, but a lodging nonetheless.

There are social realities that a minister must decide whether or not to live with and to work through when he or she is deciding whether or not to locate in the profession at all, in a particular denomination, in a particular parish. Analogously, there are social realities that a minister must decide whether to live with and to work through when deciding whether or not to locate in a particular role expectation of a particular person. When faced cleanly and openly, the social realities and limits of the profession, denomination, or parish usually can be accepted and worked with but carefully allowed not to exert sovereignty. Just because they are not faced openly and cleanly, the social realities and role expectations in the casual, informal calls are often allowed both to exert a sovereignty and to evoke bitter defiance. The suggestion here is simple: Face just as openly and deliberately and freely the limited and limiting role expectations in the daily demands and denials of more informal encounters between minister and person. Accept these calls, too, as occasions or locations for ministry, without fearing that they are sovereign blueprints for ministry.

A call to ministry is like a seed, about which Jesus talks so much. It is held carefully, because it is precious and full of life, not because it is fragile or weighted with threat. It needs to be planted, and that means it must find rooting in one place, one limited and specific piece of turf, not necessarily the most fertile. It also needs to break open. The seed will never be the same again as it emerges into the new and fuller life once locked within.

Typically, ministers resist accommodations vigorously. When the people say, "No, we won't accept you in the role and mission you have cast for yourself," ministers often respond as violently as the disciples ventured: "Lord, may we call down fire from heaven to burn them up?" And when the people say, "You must…," ministers often turn away and turn back as stubbornly as did those to whom Jesus said, "Follow…" This resistance, like any, invites exploration.

Ministers resist accommodation. This is partly because ministry needs to resist accommodation and confinement; ministry must constantly explode the niches into which people would cache it and their own lives. This is the proper ministry of the one who healed when not authorized, plucked grain when hungry, even on the Sabbath, disappointed the Palm Sunday fans, overturned the temple way of life, and constantly frustrated the disciples' presumption to be understanding Jesus and pinning him down. Ministry is in breaking out of accommodations, the ministry of one who has nowhere to lay his head. But these restraints can be erupted only from the inside, and one must willingly, even wholeheartedly, enter the prison (if that is what it feels like) before breaking out of it. Ministers tend to resist accommodation by shaking the dust off their feet prematurely, before they have walked down the dusty road into the village.

Why do ministers resist the lodging for ministry that is proffered in particular "calls"? Is it simply that ministers must safeguard the purity of their ministry and therefore, out of hand, separate and alienate themselves from the misplacing and displacing calls, the peculiar roles into which people would cast ministry? Perhaps ministers *are* sometimes the unbending, unmoved sentries guarding the purity of their own call from the encroachment of daily calls. Perhaps ministers *are* sometimes that uncertain about the integrity of their call. But more often, I think, it is something else. It is not because ministers hold themselves aloof and remote by predisposition; it is quite the opposite.

Ministers tend to be those who are predisposed to get very easily involved in the lives of others, to be eager and willing to take up lodging wherever and whenever offered. They may frequently be guarding against too easily giving in to their own yearnings for intimacy, their own inclinations to belong, to join, to blend with the lives of others. It is not so often that ministers don't know how to settle comfortably into a proffered niche in another's abode; more often they know just how easy it is to do that, especially for themselves.

Further, I think ministers know how easy it is for them, almost so easy as to have to be guarded against. Ministers have much experience in past intimacies, in having let themselves live fully into the accommodations offered by others. They have learned that such accommodations are never as permanent or as comfortable or as satisfying as they hope and sometimes even allow themselves to expect. By theological conviction, but also by hard experience, ministers are aware of the risks of idolatry and other addictions. Ministers have come too close, in their own fantasies and in their own experiences, to yielding sovereignty to appealing invitations. They know what it is to yield to an attractive "Come on in, big boy." They know the disappointments that lie within, the promises unkept, the lonely abandonment. Ministers tend to be place-less people out of principle, and out of principle reinforced by hard experience. They know what it is to be well placed, firmly placed, or to want to be, and they know the grief that lies therein.

Look closely at the two excuses or explanations offered by those whom Jesus invited to join his journey. "Let me go and bury my father first...Let me first say goodbye to my people at home...": over-commitment to past bonds, and the grief that lies in their inevitable breaking, the grief the greater because the commitment was the greater. My past lodgings are important, and the ruptures are painful and need attention. I will follow, but there is grief in leaving the past. Ministers know this. And ministers know, too: I would follow a new call, even a meager and unpromising one, just because I am a determined follower, but I know the grief that lies ahead in that, too. If I get as committed, as invested as I know I will, it will hurt all the more when I finally get stranded, let down, as I know I will. "Let me first bury those longings for intimacy and readiness to find accommodation that have fathered my ministry." Let me do the grief work now in advance, so that I can be freer to go out on the limb you point to. Let me have a garden of Gethsemane to comprehend and gentle the pain in every call before I follow it.

But Jesus' answer is just as stark as the one he discovered in his garden of Gethsemane: The grief cannot be avoided. It is part of the package, part of the ministry, and that is good. You cannot make full commitment unless you risk the certain grief that lies within it. Ministry of the everliving God who so gloried in creation as to enter fully its groanings and absorb fully its death—such a ministry is for one who longs more passionately than anyone for sure abode, yet is ever ready to find no place to lay his or her head. Such a ministry is for one who is so energetically ready to announce the new age, the new way, to anyone and everyone, that the grief and the risks known from hard past experience, though not blinked at, seem not so freighted with care as to make one withhold from new accommodations.

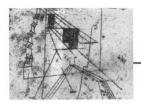

# 3

# The Empty Yes
# and the Masked Yes

*"What do you think? A man had two sons; he went to the first
and said, 'Son, go and work in the vineyard today.' He answered,
'I will not'; but later he changed his mind and went. The father
went to the second and said the same; and he answered, 'I go, sir';
but he did not go. Which of the two did the will of his father?"*
Matthew 21:28–31a

What do you think? A certain woman invited guests to a dinner party. She called one and said, "Please come," and he said, "Of course I will come! I love dinner parties, and yours especially." And indeed he came, flourishing flowers, and conversing profusely, displaying a witty opinion on every subject raised, and otherwise magnificently going through the motions of playing the charming dinner guest—and he ruined the evening for several people, even while they enviously said to themselves, "I should be able to do that." And the woman called another and invited him also. He said, "You know how I dislike dinner parties!" He came anyway, but did not venture light repartee or pretend to be knowledgeable on every subject. Instead, he more or less turned his back on the party and talked quietly and closely with only three or four people, who later said to each other, "That was a beautiful evening; I wish I could have more like that. Oh, yes, that man was nice, too." Which of these was truly present at the party and which did the will of the hostess?

What do you think? A certain man proposed marriage to a woman and promised to give her his all, and they were wed. He provided her a fine home and a high standard of living and was polite and proper and faithful and hardworking—the model husband, everyone said so. But he withheld himself—she never knew what he was thinking or feeling, if anything. And another man proposed marriage to another woman and warned her that he could give her little and probably would not be a "good husband." And, indeed, their standard of living was low, and he was not always polite and proper—sometimes they raged hard at each other—and on an occasion or two he was not faithful. But she knew his zests and pains, his dreams and frustrations, the loveliness of his bliss and the swirls of his turmoil. And they became not just one flesh but one spirit. Which of these was truly husband to his wife?

What do you think? A certain student had two teachers and went to the class of one and said, "Teach me." And the teacher lectured brilliantly, with erudition and wit. The class applauded frequently and admired the professor very much, from a distance, of course, because the professor was much too distinguished to be approached closely. And the student sitting in the seventh row looked up at the professor and wondered silently, "Where are you, and where am I in all of this display? Who are you, and who am I? I wanted you to teach me." And the student went to another class and said, "Teach me." And the professor spoke haltingly, often breaking off his lecture to sit with the students and to share musings and puzzlement. The teacher offered more questions than answers. And the student felt gripped by the contagion of the teacher's passion and curiosity. Though teacher and student soon lost touch, the student's grappling with the questions was unshakeable and lifelong. Which of these truly taught?

What do you think? A certain personnel manager was asked to comply with the affirmative action policies of his company. He meticulously completed the questionnaires required for affirmative action review by the government. He showed that each position was widely advertised and posted, that women were in fact considered among the finalists, and then he explained in great detail how each of the women did not meet the requirements of the job description as well as the men who were appointed. This demonstrated, precisely in accord with the affirmative action regulations, that it was not prejudice that kept women from the positions. Another personnel manager was impatient with these forms and these regulations, was always delinquent about completing them, and was even careless about having all openings posted on all bulletin boards. Instead, he spent a lot of time at coffee breaks—"Doesn't he ever do any work?" people said—listening to men talk about their female colleagues and secretaries and getting acquainted with the women workers. When good jobs opened, he went to some of these women and urged them to apply for positions they had not even considered. Sometimes they got them. Which of these personnel directors engaged in affirmative action? Which filled the letter and which filled the spirit of the regulations?

What do you think? Some church people wanted their minister to be "more biblical," as they said. It was a kind of "affirmative action" to make the Bible and its message more present and more meaningful in their lives. They wanted their minister to build sermons more explicitly from the Bible and to lead a group of them in weekly Bible study. The minister agreed, enthusiastically, for Bible had been his favorite subject in seminary, and he was expert in issues of biblical scholarship. He analyzed for the people the vagaries of the text, the problems of translation, and the dilemmas of trying to discover the authors' intentions—all in all, a resounding, scholarly, and astute display, emphasizing proper caution about formulating interpretations. Don't jump on any ideas. Know why you can't. (It was something like the personnel officer's complying with affirmative action regulations by explaining so carefully why it was impossible to hire a woman). Another minister, similarly asked to be "biblical," said that he had been eager to get back to the biblical religion he had grown up in, and he moved easily into quoting the Bible with a verse-long answer for any question. (Maybe this is something like a personnel officer hiring a token woman for the front office.) A third minister said the request was a very difficult one, because the Bible had always been important but never very clear to him, and the scholarship of seminary even less clear, so that he found himself still in struggle with the Bible and careless about keeping up with biblical scholarship. He opened to his people his own struggles with the Bible, that is, his sense of the urgency of its message, coupled with his sense of its elusiveness and even sometimes the irrelevance or alienation of its message. He retold the Bible's stories and read its cadences in a way that dramatized the losing struggles of the Hebrew people to be faithful, and the failure of the disciples to comprehend, and the piercing way God touched the people in the midst of these failures. Which of these ministers met the people's need to reclaim the Bible?

What do you think? "Save our marriage," a couple said to a minister. So the minister reminded them of their commitments and obligations, told them to be less self-indulgent in their grievances, to recognize the importance of marriage. The minister had them come to his office for the usual series of three conferences, recommended a weekend retreat and some books that would fortify these lessons, and finally arranged a church service in which the couple could renew their vows. So the couple was soon asking another minister, "Save our marriage." This minister said she didn't know if she could. But she sat at their kitchen table patiently, listening to one and then the other tell of pains and angers seemingly without end, and then listened to still more outbursts of anger, and then listened as the couple finally began to hear each other. So there were moments of communication, and shreds of new trust, and maybe even some hope for the marriage. Which of these ministered to the marriage?

What do you think? Some committee members asked the minister to help make their meetings more meaningful and effective. They thought, as he thought, that this meant making them more efficient. So he mobilized some techniques of administration, began calling members in advance of the meetings to ensure their attendance and to brief them on what would be discussed, drew up an agenda each time with a fixed number of minutes allocated to each item, posed the issues pro and con at the start of each discussion, intervened to cut off discussion when it began to stray, and helped the committee get through its business in record time with a sense of accomplishment: many things had been checked off and many decisions reached. But when they were finished, one took a deep breath and said, "That was like a fast train ride, and I think I missed most of the scenery." And another told her husband when she got home, "I don't remember a thing we said, but we must have said it really well, like in IBM meetings." Another committee asked their minister to help make their meetings more meaningful and effective and were initially quite frustrated at the response, for she suggested that they move away from the conference table and into the lounge and spend more time at the beginning with coffee and snacks; she seemed to turn her back on the business at hand. The minister actually pursued side tracks as they came up, and sometimes suggested that they abandon the agenda and instead spend time with new issues that burst out now and then. And one member said afterward to her husband, "I'm sorry that I'm home late, but those meetings are so gripping. It's the one committee I go to where I feel something real is happening; we're not just going through the motions. We even care enough about things to get into arguments." Which of these ministers helped make their meetings more meaningful?

## The Empty Yes

The empty yes is the routine yes, the rootless yes, the routeless yes, the yes that goes nowhere, the bodiless yes, the thin yes, the cosmetic yes, the yes that washes away at first test, the yes that crumbles at first touch and leaves the heartbreaking no. This is the yes that sabotages its promises by its own routineness, the yes that kills the spirit by feeding it the letter, the yes that defies by glibly complying. The empty yes—because it is yes—raises hopes, lulls guardedness, and lures vulnerable investment. The empty yes—because it is empty—shatters the hopes, refurbishes the guardedness, and withers the investment. The son with the ready but routine yes is seducing the father to expose his heart, so it can be broken. The minister with the routine readiness to answer people's needs and hopes is toying with these needs and hopes, sabotaging them, a friend more destructive than an enemy.

How does it feel to be a victim of the empty yes? First it feels soothingly good—a dream come true. Then it is devastating—old disappointments now cutting more deeply. It is the excruciating pain of having and not having, at once, promises raised and dashed.

When the father says, "Go and work in the vineyard," and the son says, "I go," there is new spring in the father's step, new warmth in his breast. To be a father joined by a son is like falling in love in the spring or like having one's jokes laughed at or like being called by name by a celebrity; it is like having your arguments carry the vote in a committee meeting, or like having your hand held. You are joined, recognized, embraced, confirmed. It is an experience of grace.

When the answer is yes, there is a freshening of spirit, an enlargement of self. You are jaunty, sprightly, and happy, more ready to join others because you feel joined, more ready to recognize others because you feel recognized. You are more giving, because you have been received, and more ready to receive, because you have been given to. You are more unfolded, more present, more there. It is the opposite of being lonely. It is feeling a place and a belonging.

The son's "I go" answers questions, earnest, urgent, searching questions about the relations between you and him. You wouldn't have asked if it weren't gnawingly important. You relax, more at peace with yourself and the world because this son of yours is responding as you wish and not as you feared. The yes puts to rest the gnawing suspicions of alienation and unease. Past fears and annoyances are forgotten in this new blending of wills and persons.

But the son's yes promises more than it means. It promises a fulfillment, refreshment, replenishment, a nurturing of deep hungers, a salvation. But it doesn't mean any of these things. So it is an idol and dooms your heart to anguish. It is an idol so well placed and so well promised, and you are so needy that you eagerly welcome it, rejoice, grasp, rely on it again and again. So when the idol crumbles, the grief is sore, the heart emptier than before, and the scars thick.

The empty yes breeds the empty yes: The pain of this grief over this idol failed breeds wariness and caution that becomes your own empty yes, the withholding in the affirmation you offer to others. Fatherhood frustrated by a son aloof becomes aloof father. Victims of the empty yes become performers of the empty yes. Soothed and battered by these idols, we pose as the idols that become the soothers and batterers of others. Lured and devastated by the empty yes, a minister hardens and becomes a brittle caricature of ministry. Battered by the minister's hollow, clanging, empty yes, the people learn how to charade Christian commitment too.

## The Masked Yes

There can also be chagrining enticement in the no, the masked yes: No, I will not work in the fields...but I hint I might. If the empty yes lures us into receiving, embracing as a savior, an idol that will fail us, then the hidden yes lures us into fashioning the idol. This come-on now contains a promise, but obscure, a promise withheld. So we are enticed into taking the responsibility for maturing the promise, nudging it to come true. We need to rescue the yes from its masking no. We are seduced into putting our energy into shaping the no into a yes. We rise to the challenge and build an idol, pouring into it our own energy and trust and expectations: If it/she/he says no, I can make it/her/him say yes. It *will* say yes. I will get from it in exchange for what I give, in proportion to what I give. My effort to reshape the no guarantees the yes.

This too is our story, this seduction into making "it" happen, and the painful grief when it doesn't, and then the grief-induced cautiousness with which one subsequently utters one's own yes, cloaking one's own commitments in the seductive no.

The idol of the empty yes seduces us into trusting, expecting, hoping; and its failure disappoints us into hollowing out our own yes—we make our promises glibly and smoothly—an idol that in turn, seduces, then fails, others.

The idol of the masked yes seduces us into the effort to strip away the mask, to upgrade the no into its intended yes (we're sure it is intended), and seduces us into trusting this effort, expecting, hoping; the failure of this idol disappoints us into masking, armoring our own yes—winking when we say no—a lure that seduces others into their own upgrading effort and hence their own disappointment.

This is our experience, but if we are to believe Jesus and his editors, who told the story that began this chapter, it may also be God's experience. For the father in the story seems to be intended to portray the plight of God, a father who is so eager to hear our yes, who feels so gladdened by it, that he may hear the yes well before it is matured and cannot take no as the last word, as the way people really are. If this is God's experience, the difference from our experience is not that God does not suffer, but just the opposite. God appears capable of infinite grief—this may be what makes God in fact God—without needing to fend off the pain by closing up, closing out, without needing to mute, hide, withhold, blunt the hearty yes with which God continues to address us, without either hollowing or armoring the yes. God just persists in saying and perceiving yes, until it is so.

## Victims of Yes-Sayers Become Yes-Sayers

How does it feel to be victim of the empty yes? The father gazes contentedly down across the vineyard. It is not just that the vineyard work will be done, though that is important, and he is relieved to know that the backlog of weeding and pruning will be done by the end of the day. It is also that his son loves him. That was an unspoken question within the question, "Will you help me out in the vineyard?" Now the backlog of doubts about that can be laid to rest. They do have a future together—that was another question within the question—and the father is sweetly looking forward to working alongside his son at harvest time and in the seasons ahead. The son's ready yes has eased doubts and nurtured the father, who goes about his own chores with new zest.

These contented passions of the father are the passions—filled with sure hopes—of the voter whose candidate, the one who made just the right promises, wins; of the lover whose doubts and fears are dissolved by the consenting yes that promises all will be well; of the ethnic community whose struggles at last have yielded a favorable response from city hall, the way paved for a secure future; of the war veterans who march home wearily, but triumphantly happy in the knowledge that they have won the peace that will end wars, guarantee justice, and win the gratitude of their fellow citizens; of the teacher whose student has at last seen the point, or the negotiator whose opponent has at last conceded the point; of the writer whose stubbornly slow subterranean thought processes have just yielded a plot that will now write itself; of the gardener whose patient, tender care is at last rewarded with a burst of healthy growth that will now flourish; of the distraught person whose alcoholic spouse has at last promised to go dry. All of these gaze contentedly with the father at the trusted stirrings among the vines. Patience and struggle have borne a response that buoys new covenants.

The father—each of these fathers—keeps casting his eyes down at the stirrings among the leaves and savoring the good feelings. But then toward the end of the day his eyes linger on the rustling, and a thought will not stay suppressed any longer. The father stares and stares, and the hard thought fixes in his mind. The rustling is the wind. The vineyard is empty and so was the promise and so is the father's heart, all the emptier for having burgeoned so fully. He lost a son and much more. He has lost that heartiness of self that he had invested in the son's yes. With the field empty, with the son's yes empty, part of himself is emptied, depleted, drained, hollowed.

We see the grief no more clearly than in the way the father now empties his own affirmations, the hollowness, the emptiness of his eyes expressing the emptiness of self that is grief. (Maybe—no, probably—that's how the son's yes got empty, perfunctory—it was hollowed out by his own disappointment and grief.) The father promises himself to get out to the vineyard tomorrow, but he doesn't mean it and doesn't do it. Even when he does get to the vineyards, or to any work, he does it in a routine, perfunctory way, frozen, going through the motions, dutifully doing what is required, or seeming to—zestless and soulless, for his soul is depleted. A daughter asks a question and he grunts ready acquiescence, distracted—his emptiness seeking matching shallowness—by his century's equivalent of newspaper or beer or television or home computer; but that's all she gets. His wife asks for love and he goes through the motions of giving love and speaking love, and making love. His neighbors, whose emptiness matches his and who are too depleted to ask anything of him except a casual yes, even a mocking yes, stand no more than his own tentativeness, whether at bar, cocktail party, carpool, locker room, or poker game. Poker game: The perfect symbol of the man's plight, with the false yes and the masked yes, high-stake bluff escalated to high art.

How does it feel to be victim of the come-on no, the masked yes? The father gazes down across the vineyards, calculating the work that needs doing and deciding what has to be done first and what can be put off. But he is distracted, pulled back from these thoughts about the vineyard to thoughts about the conversation with his son. There with his son, not in the vineyard, is where he feels called most urgently to labor. There's something with his son that needs doing, needs his doing. Of course he is disappointed and angry at his son's refusal, but even more he is nagged by the sense that this was not the final word. If the son's no was intended to draw attention to himself and away from the vineyard, it succeeded. The refusal was puzzling, demanding in its own way. Something was amiss that needed correction, probably his correction. His son was not himself. This was not the son the father knew, at least not the son the father wanted, dreamed. "That just wasn't like him!" The father ponders and wonders what to do. "He needs something. He needs something from me. How may I have offended him? How have I failed him?" There is something wrong here and the father feels responsible, responsible for making it wrong, responsible for making it right. The son's refusal and his retreating back have left a vacuum that draws the father in.

So the father gazes down across the vineyard, but he is thinking about the work he must do with his son, not with the vines, distracted by what the son has left unsaid more than by what he has said, and feeling challenged to get it said. What does he do? Jesus doesn't tell us, because Jesus wants to teach us about a God who doesn't have to do anything, a God who just perceives the yes that is hidden within the no, takes it for granted, deems it as so. But the earthly father needs to fill the emptiness in himself by filling the emptiness he senses in his son.

We know what he is planning as he looks down across the vineyards. The father wishes for the son's yes to be visible and the wishing becomes so earnest that it becomes the urge to control, the urge to cajole, command, plead, rebuke, whine, apologize, shame, scold, all the arts of Pygmalion, determined to pump life into the cold statue, determined to call forth his son's yes with a powerful yes of his own, hiding his anxiety behind bluster and bluff.

To be victim of the empty yes is to respond to a woman's desperate "Help!": Coach me and comfort me through this coming job interview, or school exam, or problem with my kids; teach me how to be more loving; help me through this crisis. You are unambiguously wanted, needed. There is a crucial place for you in her life. You are somebody to her, the only one she turns to. You answer with energy, commitment, and imagination, filling that place, sure of your welcome and tenure. When she gets through the crisis, you are ready to claim that place, to have that welcome and tenure confirmed, to be warmly hugged in celebration, maybe even thanks. Now you say, "Help" or "Please" or "Here I am." And she says, "Why are you so demanding or so narcissistic?" and "Can't you understand I have a new crisis coming up?" Or she turns against you, resenting your help and her dependence, and strides off. So it turns out after all that it wasn't you that she wanted, but just literally what she said, help through a crisis. So if she asks, you help with the new crisis, but it's more mechanical, more routine, more condescending—you act more like a business consultant. You miss your full-bodied zest and engagement, miss it more than she does.

To be victim of the masked yes is to stand by while the woman copes, announcing she is determined to do it herself but never quite letting you get out of sight, looking at you furtively for reassurance, sneaking a request for advice. So you sneak your response too. You let the assurance, the advice just "happen" indirectly, dropped into other conversation casually. Affirmation, praise, admirations offered, but never as though acknowledging her self-misgivings. Neither of you is honest about what is happening, so you learn to disguise yourself, to match her mask, in an arm's-length choreography. And soon you wonder where you disappeared to. It's like talking with your mouth closed, like making love with all of your clothes on. Pretending you are not there when you are becomes a pretense that you are there when you're not.

To be victim of the empty yes is to believe it when someone—colleague, spouse, friend, parent, child, minister, someone—says, "Tell me what's troubling you. Let's talk about it." So you pour it out, the dam broken by this welcome, at last, for the long-pent-up turmoil. And while the other listens, you pour and pour, grateful for the offer of a listening that is attentive and sympathetic and supportive. You know it will all be embraced by a sympathetic hug or by a warm comment or by a penetrating insight. You know that the other's invitation means he wants to know you and be with you, with all of this turmoil, not make you pretend any longer that this is not part of you, at least not with him.

Then, just when you begin to run down and pause for a breath and maybe some comfort the other says, "That reminds me of when I..." or "I'm sure that it's going to get better soon..." or "I think that what you should do is..." or "Your whole problem is..."—and you can't recognize yourself in any of these responses. So it turns out the other person, after all, like all of the rest, can't take you with all the turmoil, isn't really ready to know you as you are, wasn't seriously ready to take on all the overflow from the broken dam. So you sponge up what you can from everything that has spilled out, shore up the dam with whatever debris you can find—that is now going to take all the energy you have—and slog away.

The dam must now be stronger than ever. You don't permit yourself that many vulnerabilities to the empty yes—maybe the times you succumbed, really let go in abandon, are so long ago as to be lost. Now when people say, "Tell me..." you go through the motions, but it's routine, it's empty. You are watching yourself, controlling the spilling, vigilant to keep the dam intact, managing the charade of sharing just enough to make the other feel helpful—because it is now the preservation of the hollowed roles and the other's self-esteem and comfort, not your own nurturance, that is important here. Energy is given to preserving the forms of the yes. The empty yes takes energy; the genuine yes would have given it. In this display of energy and skill in keeping things running smoothly and evenly, you have become human again.

To be victim of the masked yes is to go to your colleague or therapist or friend or parent or minister in distress, only to have them hide from it a little, but only a little. They don't turn you away cleanly; the no is not decisive, but shallow, a come-on. They should hear you out, can, want to, but seem to need a little coaxing. "Time is a little scarce right now"; "Oh, you probably understand yourself better than I do"; "Are you sure you can trust me?" So you give them the coaxing. You accommodate them on the time, you reassure them that your demands are not great, you find ways to dose out your distress so as not to be overwhelming. You control and manage yourself to help the others play their role. You find yourself needing to encourage, perhaps even manufacture, the other's attention, the other's caring, the other's support. "You can do it," you try to persuade them; and you persuade yourself; your own flood of energy that goes into making that so, makes it so, at least for you. Once you overcome their shyness and coyness, they really are yours—the delusion of every seducer. You count on the sympathetic ear and heart you have unmasked.

From there on, it is pretty much like being the victim of the empty yes, for the yes you have uncovered is a yes you surely count on, and a yes surely empty.

To be victim of the empty yes is to feel that special elation over a new call, a new appointment. There is recognition and opportunity; your past record is affirmed, and your future is burgeoning. The search committee and the new church officers affirm the wonderful fit between you and the position. They pledge their support for your hopes and dreams.

Then you discover—the "morning after," whether it comes weeks or months later—that they meant it, but they didn't mean it. They meant what they said but didn't mean what you heard, in your long-dammed-up zest and in the sudden release of that frustration. So on the morning after there is a return to normalcy: the same old struggle for a niche and recognition for partnership, plus the hangover from the binge of celebration. And because of the hangover you walk all the more stiffly and carefully, the expansiveness and zest of the celebration turned upside down, inside out, and gutted. You don't withdraw; you are more wounded than that. You continue to say the things, but now your heart is not in it. It is a mood turned on and off quickly for just the opportune moments. It is manipulation. It is going through the motions, a hearty charade.

To be a victim of the masked yes is to be hired with an unclear job description, ambiguous responsibilities and lines of authority, uncertain symbols and mandates. They must want you—it is clear to you that they need you—but they don't seem to quite know how to say it. So you help them. You work on a job definition, and you work on selling it to them, and you work on performing in a way to match and refine the description. You create the role the way an actor or opera singer does, and you await the applause. They give you a hint of recognition now and then, often enough to encourage what you have done but also to make you aware that more needs doing. So you redouble your efforts to please, impress, to make them want you and to know you are wanted, to unmask the yes. You see yourself succeeding. All your effort and imagination do give you greater assurance. And it doesn't take much imagination to see that they recognize this too.

But that is imagination. At a meeting one evening when a favorite long-planned project is on the agenda—something you have laid the groundwork for in sermons and newsletters and in endless consultations and meetings—you suddenly hear the lay leader say, "I suppose this is an interesting idea we should talk about sometime, but let's move along to these more pressing items." Your idol, built entirely by your own efforts unilaterally, crumbles. This is your own doing—overly trustful of this idol of your own creation, expecting it to save you, when you cannot save it. But it is their doing too. In their ambiguity they have lured you, exploited you, tempted you by leaving you on your own to

49

do what you just did. They have found and tapped an old vulnerability: Be a good scout and perform well and please us, and we will love you and reward you.

So as victim you go into retreat and shelter your own enthusiasms and yearnings and commitments. You adopt a perpetual shrug, a charade of casualness and cheerfulness and cynicism. You let them go through the motions, burying deep the passion you actually feel. Some may call it burnout, but it is more like a spark still waiting to be fueled and fanned into blaze. It is frozen power waiting to be thawed. It is limpness waiting to be aroused, coaxed into action. You wait to be discovered and called forth, giving off enough hints of your talents and commitments, your yes, for those with eyes to see. But mostly, in your numbed cautiousness, you display the mask of casualness and uncaring, hiding the yes.

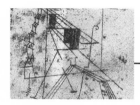

# 4

# Seeing through Expectations to Find Ministry

*One day Peter and John were going up to the temple at the hour of prayer, at three o'clock in the afternoon. And a man lame from birth was being carried in. People would lay him daily at the gate of the temple called the Beautiful Gate so that he could ask for alms from those entering the temple. When he saw Peter and John about to go into the temple, he asked them for alms. Peter looked intently at him, as did John, and said, "Look at us." And he fixed his attention on them, expecting to receive something from them. But Peter said, "I have no silver or gold, but what I have I give you; in the name of Jesus Christ of Nazareth, stand up and walk." And he took him by the right hand and raised him up; and immediately his feet and ankles were made strong. Jumping up, he stood and began to walk, and he entered the temple with them, walking and leaping and praising God. All the people saw him walking and praising God, and they recognized him as the one who used to sit and ask for alms at the Beautiful Gate of the temple; and they were filled with wonder and amazement at what had happened to him.*

Acts 3:1–10

51

The first recorded moment of pastoral ministry in the Christian church is a moment of intense mutual frustration and a moment of joyful mutual discovery, in that frustration, of fulfilling ministry.

Mutual frustration: The ministers and the beggar said no to each other. Peter and John were practicing their ministry; as was their habit, they were going to the temple to pray and were recruiting others to join them. The man declined to join them; he said no to their ministry. As was his habit, he demanded ministry in different terms, alms. They said no to that; they declined to practice ministry as he had defined it. Ministers and beggar could each feel stranded, abandoned by the other.

Mutual discovery: The apostles and the beggar took each other's no seriously. The apostles abandoned (temporarily) their path to prayer. The beggar abandoned his plea for alms. They gave up their *habits* of ministry, which failed to reach each other, and discovered that within those habits were *intentions* of ministry—for wholeness and health— that did converge. They gave up their habituated forms of ministry, and in the space thus opened they found new forms. The no-saying made them deviate from "ministry"; the deviation allowed them to find ministry. The no-saying, taken seriously, made their ministry more, not less—more faithful and true, not less; more fulfilling of intentions, not less. By the Beautiful Gate, in the openness left by abandoned prayer and denied alms, ministers and beggar discovered healing and celebrated together.

The no-saying presupposed a yes-saying. Apostles and beggar were committed to ministry but to differing and contradictory *habits* of ministry. So it is with the usual impasse between minister and people. They are both committed to ministry, genuinely committed. And they express that commitment in entrenched, habituated forms of ministry. Indeed, the earnestness of their commitment is expressed in the firmness of their habits. People less committed to ministry would be less likely to confront each other, to say no to each other, with their contradictory habits, and also less likely to feel so anguished when they *heard* a no.

In their habits the minister says, "I see ministry this way," and the people say, "No, we see ministry another way." The minister says, "I see our need and God's intended presence in our need this way." The people say, "No, we don't see our need or God's response that way. We see our need differently, and we recognize the role of God and church and ministry in our lives in quite different ways." The minister instructs the pulpit committee and the deacons and the congregation in how to be a minister of God and a church of God. And the people instruct the minister. Peter and John said, "Join us in prayer." The man at the gate said, "No, I'm not coming in; instead, give me alms." The apostles were determined in their particular new habit of ministry by the intensity of their recent experience (at Pentecost). The man was determined in his particular habit of ministry by lifelong practice. So with most ministers and people: The intensity of recent experience (as at seminary) and the entrenchment of lifelong practice firm and confirm the conflicting habits of ministry.

The minister says, "What you need and what I must do is to deepen the liturgical meaning of our worship." The people say, "No, what we need is to sing our familiar hymns; to be our minister, you must learn and lead and like them."

A man may say, "Get me a job. You know people in town and they'll listen to you, if you'll only try to help me." "No," a minister may reply. "I am here to help you get Christ. Seek first the kingdom of heaven, and these things will be added unto you."

The minister says, "You need to take God's word (and my ministry) more seriously in your lives, as with committed Bible study, or discussion of the sermon after church." The people say, "What we need is for *you* to *tell* us of God's word and for us to gather and chat after church on the front steps or over coffee."

The people say, "We need the impact in our lives that comes from having the minister call in our homes regularly, even though briefly." The minister says, "No, I can have impact where it is needed in your lives by being available regularly in my office for counseling you through crises."

The minister says, "What this community needs, and the response God wants us to make, is to develop a halfway house for ex-prisoners." The people say, "No, our community responsibility more naturally takes the form of providing space for Alcoholics Anonymous, Boy Scouts, and overflow classes from the high school."

The people say, "Can't you get my husband to stop drinking?" or "Please try to get my kids to understand how much they are hurting themselves with that junk!" The minister says, "No, I can't do that until they ask me. Tell me *your* problems."

A minister says, "We should spend at least $100 of our church scholarship money to offer a camp tuition for a kid from the inner city." A trustee says, "Tell me one good reason why we should."

The minister says, "Since you call me to be your minister, join me in these things. How can I be a minister—as I feel deeply called to be—if you will not be a church by taking your part in responding to God's call in worship and in word, in personal and community crises?" The people say, "No, how can we be a church—as we deeply and traditionally feel called to be—if you will not be our minister by taking your role in these activities?"

Such encounters are what sociologists call role conflict, what journalists call the crunch or the gathering storm, what ministers and people call impossible as they leave ministry and the church—by different doors or gates. Minister and people stay with their habits of ministry and turn away from each other, and thereby from ministry.

But by the Beautiful Gate the apostles and the beggar did not turn away from each other or from the frustrations of their encounter or from the possibilities for ministry opened by those frustrations. Each did, decidedly, turn away from their habits of ministry, their perfectly valid entrenched expectations that ministry was to be found in the sharing of prayer or in the giving of alms. But they did not turn away from the visions and yearnings lodged in those expectations. Their reaching out in prayer and in alms-asking was animated by yearnings for wholeness of life and for sharing of life. They held fast to these yearnings even while they abandoned the ministry they had supposed embodied them. The apostles yearned for all to be touched in their brokenness with the vibrant, surprising, life-giving, and faithful power of the Spirit of God they had just encountered at Pentecost. So they looked for and invited others to look for this Spirit in the gathering at prayers, where they had encountered it. The cripple yearned for remedy and for greater wholeness and looked for it (and invited others to contribute to it) in the only way he knew, alms. But then each surrendered these habituated patterns of ministry, which did not touch each other, and thereby opened the way for their yearnings to emerge and to be joined by the Spirit in a new moment and act of ministry.

Interrupting the route to prayer and denying the demands for alms, Peter took the cripple by the hand. In that sudden touching of yearnings each risked an unfamiliar and unlikely act of ministry. In sacrificing their habituated expectations of ministry, they found, together—it could not have been otherwise than together, it could not have been otherwise than in sacrifice of expectations—a surprising meeting of their yearnings in a new wholeness.

This encounter of apostles and cripple at the Beautiful Gate teaches of the call to ministry that is in the shattering of habits of ministry. This encounter at the Beautiful Gate teaches also of the call to ministry that it is in the discernment of yearnings *within* the fixed habits of ministry, yearnings revealed more easily by the shattering of those patterns.

Peter and John were not just summoners to prayer and not just deniers of alms, and the cripple was not just an abstainer from prayer and a demander of alms—although the no-saying is often all that ministers and people can hear in each other. The apostles were yearners after the wholeness of life that is nourished by living it with God. Such yearning, though obvious, is readily obscured in our times by battles over patterns of ministry. The man by the gate was a cripple, in need of God's wholeness, and presumably—long buried by habituation to his lameness and to alms—a yearner for the wholeness. This yearning, though obvious, is also readily obscured by battles over patterns of ministry.

The apostles and the beggar said no to each other. They found ministry by taking the no very seriously and listening to the positive summons lodged in the no. The apostles took the beggar's no seriously in two ways: First, they accepted it as a no to them. If he could not go with them in their patterns of ministry, if these did not meet his needs, they could give up (at least temporarily) their patterns of ministry and stay with him, in search of new ministry. This was genuine sacrifice and risky venture. That's what the no meant to *them*: a frustration of intentions and a call to sacrifice. They accepted this. Second, they were attuned to what the no meant to the beggar, to what it meant beyond merely "no." It meant that other needs were clamoring for attention and ministry, yearnings that found expression, blunt and blunted to be sure, in the no. They also found expression, still blunt and blunted, in the demand for alms. But the apostles could also take seriously their own no to the alms. Their no was a way of looking into, not a way of looking away from. To take the no seriously was to unpeel the definitions, the roles, the patterns of ministry that evoked them, and thus to open the yearnings within those patterns to greater self-consciousness and to each other. "I have no silver and gold; but what I have I give you." No to the gold is a means of discerning more clearly "what I have." No to the gold is a means of discerning more clearly the "you." The no is a prelude to matching these—"what I have" and "you"—in a new moment of ministry.

## "Peter Looked Intently at Him..."

When Peter looked at the man, what did he see? He saw a beggar, yes. He also saw a cripple. He also saw a whole man. To fix his eyes on *him*, to see him wholly, to minister to him, Peter needed to see all three.

It is too easy for the minister to see only the beggar, the one who is defining what the minister should do—in this case, give alms. Expecting a gift from them, the man was all attention. It is easy to be lured into the roles that people would define and to call that ministry; the minister may call it "relevance," and critical onlookers may say "sell-out." "I have no silver or gold..." It is easy to deny the roles that people would define and to call *that* ministry; the minister may speak of "transcendent higher callings," and the critical onlooker may say "cop-out." Peter and John could have seen only the beggar; they could have dropped in their coins, dutifully and with satisfaction, and gone on their way, never really noticing his real needs or possibilities, that he was also a cripple and also a whole man. Or they could have overlooked his begging, urging him to come to prayer and feeling satisfaction from *that*; again not noticing his needs or possibilities, not seeing that he was a cripple or a whole man, which were signaled by his begging.

When vocational identity—call—is uncertain or under challenge, then it is especially tempting to don the role expectations of others, especially when these are as firmly entrenched in habit and culture as almsgiving, making moral and biblical pronouncements, saying grace at women's fellowship and Kiwanis luncheons, or supporting gospel hymns and Boy Scouts. Whether we comply or defy, if all we can see is the expectation, then we cannot see the needs and the possibilities it points to.

55

The minister needs to see but also to see through the expectations others have for ministry. Peter and John could see the man as cripple and as whole man precisely because they could see him as beggar. "Peter looked intently at him." Peter could recognize and accept him so unambiguously as beggar that he could see through the begging and see him whole. The apostles could see the man's expectations for ministry so clearly that they could say no to those expectations and minister to him.

There were bystanders by the Beautiful Gate. Almsgiving is what they all expected, and when the apostles insisted on seeing through the alms-asking and almsgiving to recognize and respond to the needs signaled by the alms-asking—to see the man as cripple and as whole—they offended the crowds and precipitated stormy dispute with the authorities. Ministry lies precisely in seeing through the façades, in exposing and exploring and changing questions more than in giving answers, in enlarging quest and demand more than in fulfilling settled and conventional role expectations. Ministry is in seeing through what others see as a matter of course, what others accept blindly, and this is never more true than with the expectations of ministry that others hold routinely. These expectations are tempting, for they do provide models of ministry, and they are well entrenched and acceptable in church and culture. Almsgiving would have done *something* for the man, and it was what everybody expected. But these expectations are challenging and need to be challenged just because they are others' expectations, the world's expectations, the devices worked out by the world to heal itself, the devices that therefore perpetuate the brokenness as much as heal it. The giving of alms, what everyone expects, measures and continues the crippledness but does not heal it. Alms demean the man, confirm him in his lameness, and in fact become the very measure of the distance between his state and health. Peter and John, refusing to measure out with alms this distance between him and them, the distance between brokenness and wholeness, saw the man as already participating with them in a world of vigor and wholeness. They insisted on proclaiming what they saw, by joyful deed and joyful word, together.

But the minister who ventures to live and to proclaim this more penetrating vision of wholeness represents a world alien to the broken world that is calling for ministry. That alienation is precisely why one ministers, but it is also precisely what ruptures ministry, the rupture of trying to represent wholeness to a world of brokenness. The world of brokenness confronts ministry, not only with its ills but also with the prescriptions and remedies it has tried to devise for its ills, prescriptions and remedies that represent the brokenness and confirm it.

Society as a whole, not just needy individuals at the temple gate or the church assembled within, extends its hand and its definition of temptingly precise and gratifyingly recognized forms of ministry. Recognizable and recognized healers in our culture are physicians, psychiatrists, social workers, psychologists, counselors, maybe in special ways people like city planners and teachers—all members of established professions, as established as responses to disease in our culture as almsgiving was in another. It is natural for a minister to try to find call—established vocational identity—by alliance with or imitation of one of these professions. But these professions, and the very notion of professionalization, are ways that the world has devised to respond to its own ills, and, as a consequence, they participate in and perpetuate the ills as much as they mitigate them. The very professional status that provides the minister with the secure role definition preserves the "client's" role definition of insecurity. The exalted status of the professional enhances the client's sense of alienation and separation from healing and from agents of healing. The same professionalization that accords the minister new identity imprisons the clients with newly circumscribed and prescribed definitions of their situation. They become "patients" or "clients" and assume those "problems" that the social worker or psychological counselor or ministerial imitator is prepared to solve. They are to that degree closed off from a more complete understanding of their situation. When seen only as beggars, they see themselves only as beggars. In aspiring to and accepting the professional status that society affords, the minister participates in and perpetuates a depersonalization that is one of the principal ills of society and of those whom he or she would heal. The giving of alms measures rather than heals the illness.

We are called to be ministers by the intentions of God for his broken world. He intends his people to be whole, and he is at work to make us whole. Because we are his, we, too, work toward wholeness for all. But because we are also broken members of an alienated world, God's call is not enough for us. The world and our inner brokenness compel us to identify our ministry and to measure it, and the terms we borrow from the world to measure by are the tasks of doing well and doing good. When we are at the task of enabling others to do good (by coaching them with pronouncements of the good and the good ways to achieve it) and when we are at the task of enabling others to do well (coaching and goading them to successful performance of prescribed social roles), then we are doing well, and in that we can claim a professional role, one recognized by the world and therefore by us. So our calling to be ministers of God becomes embodied in the professional role definitions of the world, as these are lodged in us and as they are lodged in all those about us who give them compelling voice. We use the world's acclaim for good works to identify and justify our self. To establish our own vocation, we contort our true vocation: the call to be one of God's people.

Yet ministry must remain in the world, even though not of it, especially ministry in the name of the Incarnate Lord. So Christian ministry proceeds by a kind of stumbling, crunching rhythm, accommodating itself to the terms of the culture and the world it would yet transform ("To the weak I became weak, so that I might win the weak. I have become all things to all people, that I might by all means save some" [1 Cor. 9:22]), yet stoutly resisting—by seeing through—the terms of the world it would nevertheless move easily among ("Do not be conformed to this world, but be transformed by the renewing of your minds" [Rom. 12:2]).

"Get me a job. You know people in town, and they'll listen to you if you'll only try to help me." In this demand and definition of ministry, the minister may see a chance to be effective in a way that can be measured by the helped individual and acclaimed by the community. "Now you are showing that ministers can really do something useful." So the minister may scurry off to find the job and feel gratified at this "new form of ministry in a secular age."

Or the demand may be seen as pure distraction from ministry. The minister may summarily dismiss or refer the request or even locate a job, in order to quickly get back to the preaching or Bible study or prayer or whatever is construed as true ministry, letting it proceed untouching and untouched by the demand for the job.

Or it is possible to fix our eyes, to look so closely and carefully at the demand for the job as to take it seriously and to see through it, to see what needs and possibilities for ministry are signaled by this demand. The demand for help in finding a job is more likely a symptom of brokenness than it is a prescription for remedy. To help find the job feeds that symptom more than it heals. Almsgiving confirms the lameness. For a man to come to the minister and ask for this help in finding a job is to afford the minister a good glimpse of what is wrong, not of how it can be made right.

If there are jobs to be had for the minister's asking (a genuine shortage of jobs would be a different case), then presumably there are also jobs for the man's asking. His plea for help becomes a measure of…what? Maybe his own sense of inadequacy, maybe his desperate fears of facing risks, maybe rigid defense against facing any realistic self-appraisal, maybe avoidance of other distresses by insisting that the job is the problem, maybe a revealingly idolatrous addiction to work, maybe a desire to capture the minister (and God?) to his bidding. We don't know until we get past his definition of ministry. ("I have no silver and gold.") Or more accurately, we won't know what his definition for our ministry means to him until we get past what it means to us.

But we can be reasonably sure that in his demands are more clues to his ailing than to his healing, clues to the difficulties he had in holding a job and undoubtedly to other distresses in his life. These clues can become occasions of healing ministry. But so long as we accept his definition of ministry, offer the alms he asks, and move on, we can never help him perceive or experience the world in which he could walk—no matter how much genuine gratitude he may feel for generous alms and how much acclaim bystanders may shower on us.

"Can't you get my husband to stop drinking?" "Please try to get my kids to understand how much they are hurting themselves with that junk!" Drug abuse, by whatever generation, is a real problem; and when the abuser asks for help, that will be one occasion for important ministry. When the wife or father asks the minister to shape up another person, that is something else. The alms they ask may help. The minister may scurry off on the assigned mission to reform the husband or the kids, and any partial success or even the effort will certainly win community acclaim and fervent personal gratitude. But it will not heal the lameness or hear the yearning in the asking.

The minister may, quite accurately, recognize that effective ministry to the abuser cannot begin with spouses' or parents' wishes and therefore summarily dismiss the request: "No, I can't do that until they ask me. But I will listen while you tell me your problems." But this will not heal the lameness or hear the yearning in the asking either.

What lameness may be seen in and through the asking? Anger at abandonment? Fear of censure, public or self-administered, for failure as wife or father? Fear of joining in such self-indulgence? Maybe some of the same impatience with deviation or intolerance of others' distress that has contributed to the husband's or child's abuse? Turning to the minister is part of the larger brokenness of the family, of which the drug abuse is also part, just as alms-asking is part of what defines the cripple. And we can call the cripple to health only when we see the crippledness in the alms-asking as much as in the lame legs. Then we can move beyond, to ministry of healing.

"Tell me one good reason why we should spend at least $100 of our church scholarship money to offer a camp tuition for a kid from the inner city." Here the definition of ministry—"tell me one good reason"—is less dramatic than the demand for a job or for moral reform of relatives and is obscured by the controversy over the budget item. Nevertheless, the minister, in this case, is being instructed in how to play her role in that controversy: supply reasons. This is one of the most conventional roles—making pronouncements—to which ministers are assigned. The minister is more than ready to comply, predisposed by all the other expectations—of the liberals on the Christian education committee, of the seminary professors, of her husband, of all those who would charter and acclaim ministry in the form of "giving reasons." Win or lose the $100 budget item, win or lose the trustee, a vigorous ministry of giving stalwart reasons will be admired and gratifying. It also will not address whatever special possibilities for ministry are lodged in the form of this request.

Or the request for reasons may be simply recognized as the distraction and the obstacle that it is, in the way of the modest plan for the church to contribute to an individual from the inner city. "Let's talk about that later." "Let's get on with the rest of the budget and the vote." "I intend to preach about this next month." "I'll give you an article I read that may help." Defying the demand may also be gratifying to the minister and to onlookers, but it, like complying, does not address whatever possibilities for ministry may be lodged in this form of this request.

The request, trivial and distracting as it may seem, can nevertheless be seen through to ministry. It can be recognized as a symptom. Such reasoning and debating partakes more of divisiveness than of the wholeness of the community and the individuals within it. It partakes more of the preoccupation and protection of self and of "mine" than of sharing life with others. It participates more in the justification of self than in humiliation of self. It must be that the same constriction of outlook that prompted the fear of spending $100 "outside" also prompts the form of the question ("Can we justify this?"). To respond to the question in its terms, to supply the arguments, to make one faction of the church prevail over another faction—this mode of behavior confirms and feeds the constricted outlook it would profess to undo.

There are other ways of identifying and responding to the apprehensions and constrictions present in the trustee's demands. But they all presuppose resisting his definition, and probably also the Christian education committee's definition, of the minister's task at the time. And they all presuppose the minister's ability to transcend the confining terms of the meeting and to see the trustee as one who can walk forth upright as an adult among other adults despite his present cowering behind a narrow demand for narrow ministry. The minister can find ways to say "Let's talk about this later" that seem to take the request, and the trustee, seriously, not dismissing it and him. The minister can cut through the petty debate and say, wholeheartedly and warmly, as in this case she did, "Oh, we are too good friends to have to pretend that we are in a debating society or a courtroom. You've been a tightwad for twenty years with the church's money; we all know that and thank you for it. We wouldn't be where we are today if you weren't. But we also know that you have a lot of trouble, more than you want even, seeing what's important about relating to the people in the inner city. Maybe you always will, but I hope not. And I think maybe you hope not, too. Let's not take time for 'reasons' now. Maybe you will or won't approve this $100 item.

But let's save the time and I'll take you out to camp next month and make you meet the kid."

## "Look at Us…What I Have I Give You"

But all of this is only half of what is to be learned about ministry at the Beautiful Gate. This has been about people's expectations for the minister and how they can be broken open and seen through, frustrated even while taken seriously, in order to find space and focus for ministry. The almsgiving was recognized and denied so that the cripple and the whole man could be recognized. But the apostles, too, had expectations that had to be broken open and seen through so that the yearnings and intentions within *those* expectations could be released and meet the man's. "Peter fixed his eyes on him." Peter turned aside from his course for prayer, wholeheartedly turned aside and *fixed* his attention on the *man*. He abandoned, for the time being, his appointment for prayer but not his mood of joyful faith in God's gracious power, which the prayer was to express. Indeed, he abandoned his appointment for prayer in order to unlock and disclose just that joyful faith in God's gracious power. It became more abundant and available in the breaking of the appointment than it would have been in its keeping. The minister's expectations no less than the man's had to be broken open and seen through so that the yearnings in each could meet in ministry.

Long-time, entrenched, established habits and patterns and appointments of ministry, which a minister brings to any situation, are no less tempting and no less challenging and no less in need of challenge than are the demands that people seem to impose on the minister. They are no less symptoms of brokenness, nor are they any less signals of possibility, vessels of promise. The minister's expectations are bolstered, too, often from the past. Going to the temple to pray, like almsgiving, was what everybody expected and approved. So with helping people to "get Christ…to seek first the kingdom of heaven" (even when opposed to helping people get jobs) or with talking to people about their own problems or with pushing through a $100 tuition. So, too, with developing halfway houses and with reserving time for crisis counseling and with renewal of the worship service. But all of these perfectly legitimate calls need to be set aside on occasion, on the occasion when they run athwart conflicting demands that would call forth from these calls the *call* they signal. But it is especially when call—vocational identity—is uncertain or under challenge, especially in these occasions of thwarting, that a minister clings most tenaciously and desperately to those forms of call that give expression to, even as they obscure, the fundamental yearnings and commitments of his or her ministry.

"We should spend at least $100 of our church scholarship money to offer a camp tuition for a kid from the inner city." The minister's proposal expresses well a fundamental commitment and yearning for wholeness among God's people. The proposal is all the trustee can see, just as alms-asking is all some ministers can see. Can the minister behave in such a way that the trustee can "see through" the proposal and experience the yearning for wholeness within it? She can, as many ministers do, stick firmly to the proposal as the best way of expressing that commitment and yearning, and thereby prevent the trustee from discerning and ex-periencing it. Or she can abandon the proposal, either under fire or by returning the fire, and thereby again prevent the trustee from discern-ing and experiencing the commitment to wholeness that the proposal signals. Or she can hold to the proposal but loosely enough to leave room for the trustee to see more than just the proposal and for her to express her commitment for wholeness of community. This is what she seems to have done in the rejoinder quoted earlier. She was ready to forsake for a time her own proposal, just as she was ready to forsake for a time the trustee's demands for reasons. And in the room left by that forsaking, the minister was able to bespeak and enact more wholeness, in the trustee, in the trustees' meeting, and between the trustee and the inner-city kid, than she could have by insisting on the proposal to which she had, thirty minutes earlier, been insistently committed as a crucial expression of wholeness. So it is a *mutual* frustration of expectations— the "Me, too" readiness of the minister to be off balance and vulnerable, deprived of the comfort and security of conventional roles, that permits ministry. If the minister can let go and open up, then perhaps the people can too. But the mutualness is more focused than that. Since they share the moment of confrontation, they share a lot. If habitual expectations of ministry are colliding, then the commitments and yearnings embodied in those expectations are in touch, and at some point they must converge.

The minister says, "What you need and what I must do is to deepen the liturgical meaning of our worship." The people say, "No, what we need is to sing our familiar hymns." It looks like a classic impasse, min-ister and people saying a resolute no to each other's patterns and expectations of worship. But only the slightest effort is needed to see through these conflicting expectations and discern the converging and mutual yearnings and intentions within them. Both are seeking genuine and meaningful religious experience. The more formal liturgy has been meaningful for the minister, has made contact with the resources of com-munity and heritage and symbol, has made God more vividly and vitally present. The familiar hymns have put the people in touch with the re-sources of community and heritage and symbol that make God more vitally and vividly present to them. Both want to reconfirm and enhance the memory of genuine religious experience, one through the continu-ities of a sung psalm, the other through the continuities of "The Old Rugged Cross."

When they say no to each other's preferences, it seems at first as though they are saying no to the yearnings. It can be, and usually is, a time of hurt and frustration and battle and rupture of ministry. But if they can—it is the minister's role to lead this heeding—fix their eyes firmly on each other, take each other's expectations seriously enough to see through them and to discover the common yearning, then the confrontation becomes a time of blended ministry: Although your ways are not my ways, and my ways are not your ways, we want the same things.

In one church just such a moment of impasse yielded a startling new sense of community, some fresh symbols, and a striking feeling of the creative and redemptive power of God. In good humor and trust the minister and the people said to each other: "Look, when you come right down to it, for us in this suburb, nearing the twenty-first century, there are forms potentially richer than either a chanted psalm or 'The Old Rugged Cross.'" They even disbanded the choir, and those who had needed the choir now found some of their needs better met in the team that every Thursday evening (formerly choir practice night) planned the coming week's worship, and some other needs were met in introducing and explaining the Sunday worship to their congregation each week. The church happened to turn mostly to guitar music, some recorded and some live, and to other forms that may prove to have even a shorter life span than did chanted psalms and evangelical hymns. But the church will be ready when the time comes again to say no.

Meanwhile, the sharing of the no and the impetus it gave to new community and newly meaningful worship was symbolized, crudely but most intimately, in a moment the committee included in the morning worship about once a month: The minister started to chant a psalm, which was the cue for the congregation to begin singing "Let the Lower Lights Keep Burning." And the counterpart resolved, after "You may rescue, you may save," into a joyful singing of "Amazing Grace," which for this congregation was a fresh and striking hymn. The ritual was a bit corny but genuine, and it always evoked spirited participation, much turning of heads, and exchanging of smiles. It was indeed effective celebration of the real life this community discovered when expectations of worship were disrupting and disrupted to make room for new experiences of worship that made God more vividly and vitally present.

The apostles, deterred from their prayers, refusing alms, took the hand of the man and said, "In the name of Jesus Christ of Nazareth, walk."

"Intense crisis counseling," the minister says; and the people say, "No, regular brief home visits." The scene is the last regular deacon's meeting of the year, this minister's first year in the church, and the minister is making a report of his pastoral work. He wants the deacons to know that he is now spending between five and ten hours a week in intense pastoral counseling with members of the church, and two or three hours a week with nonmembers. People stop in his office, by appointment, for an hour or an hour and a half, usually every week or every two weeks. He wants to tell the deacons this because they probably wouldn't know it otherwise—this part of ministry is quiet and confidential—and because it is something of considerable satisfaction, even pride, for the minister. He has invested much training and experience; he goes to an annual summer workshop in psychological and psychiatrically oriented training for clergy. He is persuaded that it is crucial for clergy to be able to offer this professional expertise and is delighted that even in his first year he has developed the reputation and trust that nourish this kind of counseling ministry.

But the minister's enthusiasm is hardly echoed by the deacons. There are a couple of polite "That's interesting" remarks, and one deacon asks, with genuine uncertainty and curiosity, not with hostility or humor, "You just sit and talk like we are doing, or do you use a couch or something?" They see—or fail to see—this intense counseling only at face value (as the apostles might have seen the man at the gate only as an alms-asker, or the man might have seen the apostles only as prayer-bound). And the minister *could* see this coolness, at face value, as resistance to this important ministry.

But the minister is willing and able to invite them to fix their eyes on each other and see through this initial face-off. He looks squarely at their subtle no-saying and invites them to do likewise, so they can open it up and understand what it encodes. "I don't exactly see you all lining up at my door, and maybe you are wondering why anybody does." The minister speaks with the same directness yet openness that has earned him the trust and developed the counseling ministry he has just been speaking of. And the deacons respond in the same way as those who have come for counseling: "Well, that probably doesn't leave you time for other things, or for other people at least." "I guess we are a little more used to ministers who come out to see us rather than ask us to come see them." "This would really be good, for you to tell everybody how much of this you do. When we don't see you in our homes very much, we can easily forget that you *are* seeing some of us." The minister is hearing a familiar complaint and expectation: Call in our homes regularly, like ministers always have, or you aren't really being our minister.

But instead of seeing these complaints only as complaints, which might make him either defensive or compliant, he tries to fix his eyes— and the deacon's—firmly on the complaints, so as to see through them. "I hear you loud and clear. You miss it, or think some of the people miss it, that I don't get out into the homes more often and more regularly."

"Well, there's something special about having the minister in the house, even if he doesn't stay there long." Or, "One of my earliest memories is having the minister stop in for tea when I was a little boy. That always seemed to make supper special after that, and he always had a nice word for me too." Or, "Some things shouldn't change, even when everything else does, or maybe especially when everything else does." Or, "We all need some attention, not just the squeaky hinges. Sometimes it just doesn't feel right to call up and make an appointment to see your minister, like he was a doctor or someone; that's like making an appointment to see your wife." Soon the deacons are talking, relatively comfortably, about some of the concerns that were encoded in their coolness to the idea of intensive crisis counseling for the few. A sociologist who was listening might speak about alienation, about the anxiety over loss of stable and intimate and familiar ties to significant people and to significant values. The ebbing quality of their life seems symbolized and worsened by the apparently increasing professional remoteness of the minister. The minister they need is a member of the family, a very special member of the family, not a skilled professional.

The minister gives ear and gives voice, a discerning and a compassionate voice, to these complaints-become-confessions, in a way that is both like a member of the family and like a skilled professional.

But that is not all the minister does. It is the minister's own strong commitment—perhaps, one might even say, addiction—to formal and intensive and personal counseling that has started the conversation. It is not fair or ministerial, although perhaps it is "professional," to turn the analysis only on the deacons. If there is a second mile to go, one ought to go with them. So he offers a "Me, too" confession to invite all others to fix their eyes on the minister. Let them help the minister see through the strong habits of ministry.

The minister gradually comes to realize and to share such self-recognition as this: "I know what you are talking about when you talk about the 'specialness' of having the minister in your house, and also when you talk about how hard it seems to be these days to get really close to people that you want to get close to, and also when you talk about feeling left out, as when you feel the minister is slighting some members of the parish for a kind of elite corps of counselees. I feel that same kind of need for specialness, especially in personal relations, and I guess that's one thing that makes me comfortable with intense and prolonged personal counseling. We do get down to special things, and we do get close to each other in ways that don't seem to happen so much when I stop by the house for coffee or whatever. It may be true that I am looking for some of the same things in this counseling ministry that you are looking for when you ask me to call in your homes. I also know what it means to feel left out, I think, because any new minister coming into a settled congregation feels kind of like an outsider, and as often as I may call in your homes, this still doesn't go away too easily. So I suspect that I cast around for my own special circle of people I can feel more easily that I belong with, and I suppose that's one thing I get out of these more intimate and more intense counseling relationships. This is a confession; it shouldn't be that way, but I am just telling you that I think I can understand, in my own way, what you are talking about."

Some of the deacons seem taken aback by this fixing of eyes and seeing through; they are more accustomed to, and feel more comfortable with, leaving things at face value and arguing, politely, about church policies and calling schedules and the like. But most deacons are energetically and unself-consciously involved, on the edges of their chairs, experiencing a rare moment of intimacy and sharing, an honest openness. Suddenly, one blurts out, "We are talking about sharing and about specialness and about getting together—and here we are doing it!" Before long, they are making commitments, which they mean and mostly are able to keep, to have a discussion at every deacons' meeting in the coming year about what they decide to call, straightforwardly, "what the church really means to me." In the course of the following year there is less formal intensive office counseling than in the preceding year and much less restless demand for visiting in the home. Instead, there is more of the ministry that each was pointing to.

Can there be a sense of ministry and of healing that is freed of the futile and self-defeating scramble for defined roles and yet is still credible? Can a minister truly abandon the search for defined status, articulated identity, professional roles and, by the terms of such criteria as these, be nothing and still be minister? Indeed, can one be a minister just because he or she is "nothing"? Is there any recognizable role-less role, identity-less identity? Or must such talk be limited to ordination rhetoric—ministry of faith and not of self-justifying good works, commitments and calling that transcend the social- and self-reward system that sanctions roles and professionalization, healing gospel ministry of joyful self-abandon? Is there really a style or mood of ministry that forsakes roles and in that forsaking becomes ministry?

If we contemplate such a style of self-abandonment in ministry, a ministry without role definition, do we feel this to be a weakness and an emptiness, an unjustified status, as it seems in the eyes of the world? ("What *do* you ministers do to earn your money?") Or can we credibly claim such a style as a positive, vigorous selfhood and ministry of a new order, perhaps of a new age? Can it be such even though the world (and therefore many of us much of the time) cannot recognize it?

"But whoever loses his life for my sake, he will save it." Mightily as we struggle to define ourselves, establish ourselves, justify ourselves with our measured and measurable doings, we only succeed in establishing our brokenness. Our role as minister does not come into being by our efforts to minister. If our being is not to be found up the stepped path of our doings, dare we seek it down the steep, risky path of nonbeing?

# PART TWO

---

**pressure,** n. 1. a pressing or being pressed; compression; squeez-ing. 2. a condition of distress; op-pression; affliction. 3. a compel-ling influence; constraining force. 4. demands requiring immediate attention; urgency.

# The Pressure
# of Ministry

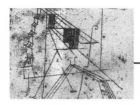

# 5

# Who Am I
# That I Should Go?

*Moses was keeping the flock of his father-in-law Jethro, the priest*
*of Midian; he led his flock beyond the wilderness, and came to*
*Horeb, the mountain of God. There the angel of the LORD ap-*
*peared to him in a flame of fire out of a bush; he looked, and the*
*bush was blazing, yet it was not consumed. Then Moses said, "I*
*must turn aside and look at this great sight, and see why the bush*
*is not burned up." When the LORD saw that he had turned aside*
*to see, God called to him out of the bush, "Moses, Moses!" And*
*he said, "Here I am." Then he said, "Come no closer! Remove the*
*sandals from your feet, for the place on which you are standing is*
*holy ground." He said further, "I am the God of your father, the*
*God of Abraham, the God of Isaac, and the God of Jacob." And*
*Moses hid his face, for he was afraid to look at God. Then the*
*LORD said, "I have observed the misery of my people who are in*
*Egypt; I have heard their cry on account of their taskmasters.*
*Indeed, I know their suffering…So come, I will send you to*
*Pharaoh and bring my people, the Israelites, out of Egypt." But*
*Moses said to God, "Who am I that I should go to Pharaoh to*
*bring my people, the Israelites, out of Egypt?"*

Exodus 3:1–7, 10–11

In the often lifelong throes of trying to discern God's call with confidence and clarity, most of us are likely to envy Moses: "If only I had
seen what he saw and heard what he heard, then I would know!" But
the biblical account makes clear that the burning bush and vivid summons by God were still not enough. Moses still balked.

"Who am I that I should go?…What shall I say to them?…Behold,
they will not believe me or listen to my voice…I am not eloquent…but I

am slow of speech and of tongue…Oh my Lord, send, I pray, some other person" (Ex. 3, 4 passim).

The insecurity and self-doubt are uncomfortably familiar, that easy preference to defer ministry until training and talent are adequate, until faith and sense of call are firm, until we feel prepared.

However, though Boy Scouts and U. S. Marines can aspire to "be prepared," ministers cannot. By definition, call comes as disruption, intrusion, displacement, knocking us out of routines, because the routines need remedy.

Moses' unexpected summons took him by surprise. Maybe if he had had a little more notice, a little more time to prepare, a chance to fit it into his thinking and his schedule, maybe if he, like the stalwart religious man walking up the Jericho road past the fallen traveler, hadn't been preoccupied with other demands, maybe if he could have had a few courses, or a chance to "talk it over with someone," maybe a short in-palace training program on ministry to Pharaohs—then *maybe* he could have responded more positively, with, as we say these days, less "role-conflict" or less "passive-dependency."

But Moses *was* taken by surprise. He had left Egypt, where the important action was, and was tending sheep in the wilderness. That is hardly a place where you expect to find the Lord, especially if you are in Moses' position and haven't read past Exodus to know how often that is just exactly where he and occasion for ministry are found, in the ordinary and remote and unexpected and lowly, among people going about their daily affairs. The Lord seldom appears or summons in those occasions for which we are so carefully and confidently prepared. And when we are taken by surprise, Moses speaks for all of us in making excuses and stalling for time, and for a greater sense of confidence and competence. "Who am I that I should go?…What shall I say?…They will not believe me or listen to my voice…I am not eloquent…Oh, my Lord, send, I pray, some other person." "Call me next week, or next year, but I can't see my way clear to it this time." Meanwhile, in moratorium—for a lifetime.

Perhaps you are ready to discuss the redemptive actions of God with confidence, perhaps even with brilliance, in the sermon or study group for which you have prepared. Perhaps you have learned how to "do" pastoral counseling, at its regularly appointed time and place, in fifty minutes of standardized give and take. Perhaps, given time to reflect on others' discussion, you come up with helpful suggestions on social action at the Council of Churches committee meeting.

But then there are those burning bushes that compel you to turn aside from the familiar path. They come so often in the wilderness, just when you leave the busy action in Egypt, just when you have completed the checklist of things you *have* prepared for. Your seat partner on the plane discovers you are a minister and suddenly takes this so seriously that he pours out the pent-up question: What must I do to be saved? On vacation, you are suddenly ushered to the side of a dying man because he wants a minister and you're the only one around. Then his widow turns to you. You are finally locking the parish house on Sunday evening after a long day, and there in the shadows of the front steps is a high school girl waiting to pour out her turbulent confessions. A neighborhood is caught up in a swirling and bitter crisis, and there you are in it—just where you should be able to relax. What started out as a routine welcoming call on new residents soon exposes bitter rancor in the family, with man and woman snapping at each other and asking, almost explicitly, for pastoral mediation. Then there is the sneering adolescent boy you encounter on what started out to be an informational guided tour of the detention home or the man who wants to know, after your carefully balanced statement from the pulpit, how you really think he should vote in the coming election.

These are the burning bushes so intense that we, too, turn our faces away—not nearly so much in cowardice as in honest recognition of the stark limitations of our puny resources. "Who am I that I should presume to meet this call?" "I just prayed I would have it in me." "I felt like an imposter. They were looking to me and really expecting me to do something about it." "Oh, my Lord, send, I pray, some other person." "It's a good thing I'm still in training (or still in my first pastorate) (or have signed up for the summer refresher course). When I get to be a real minister I can handle things like this." "It's a good thing I know a psychiatrist who does know how to handle these things (or a social worker, or psychologist, or a senior minister…)." "I should write the seminaries that they should have a course on *this* kind of problem, because I feel so unprepared for it."

So we live in a moratorium or exile of our own making, a kind of deferment—we refuse to say "exemption" for we see it as only temporary—from full ministry. This interim mood is compounded of despair, of hope in its overcoming, and a kind of scramble to hasten the overcoming.

But this scurrying for assurance only leads us farther into the wilderness, the wilderness of contrived evidence of assurance, the wilderness of those signs and wonders that lead us away from, rather than toward, what they would point to. Moses asked for concrete evidence of his authority and God's support, and he got instead a rod full of magic powers. The Jewish people later succumbed to the same temptation and built for themselves a golden calf. Then they built an ark and a temple and an intricate legal system to contain this awesome God of the burning bush, to make God manageable. For ministers, the assuring evidence of readiness for ministry may be sought in the signs and wonders of professionalism, of smoothness and poise, of a battery of techniques, of well-defined roles, or else in the signs and wonders of concrete results to be tallied, people and dollars to be counted. But this search for assurance, before we start, leads us farther into the wilderness, because we become so burdened down with the tools of preparation and badges of merit that we lose our way and forget what we were about.

"Who am I that I should go?"

The Lord's answer to Moses: "But I will be with you."

This is, first of all, a rebuke. Who are you to be saying, "Who am I?" You may have problems about identity or many other things. But this has nothing to do with whether or not you should go. It has nothing to do with whether your mission will be effective. Take off your shoes. You are standing on holy ground. Take off the anxiety and fussing you usually wear and enjoy as part of yourself. This is different from your usual worries about achieving and about pleasing other people. This is the Lord who is calling you, and who is with you. Of course it is natural to be concerned about establishing rapport with the seat partner, the high school girl, the bickering family, and all the rest, to be worried about gaining their acceptance, and to be showing a congenial "acceptance" toward them. Of course it is natural to be concerned about one's own self-acceptance, to be able to leave one of these encounters and feel the satisfaction of having done something helpful (or at least of having done something right—those seminary professors may still be lurking over your shoulder). But don't be so presumptuous as to confuse these natural but personal concerns with the question of God's acceptance of you or of another, or with the question of the achievement of God's purposes. God has little need of these personal relationships or personal satisfactions, which we have so much need of. They hardly provide reliable indices of the presence of God or of the accomplishment of his purposes. This is the grossest kind of anthropomorphism, to project upon God the face of those parents, professors, parishioners, or others whose approval and praise is important.

If I pray that I may have it in me to serve, my prayer is an offense: I betray my concern to justify myself. If I feel like an imposter, I am—not because my resources are so feeble but because the pretensions betrayed by this feeling are so high. Where do I get the idea that I am looked to to be more than I am? It is illusion and pretension to suppose that we will ever be more ready than we are now, that our faith will ever be surer, our vocation clearer, our competence more established (just as it is an illusion to wait for the circumstances to be more glorious or propitious than now). Our limitations as human servants to the living God are far more radical and essential than we so glibly claim when we say, "Wait until next year." Christ sent his disciples forth with nothing but the promise that "What you are to say will be given to you" (Mt. 10:19). Do you really think that *you* are going to do any healing of persons or peoples—now or in the future?

"I will be with you" is a rebuke also because it reminds us that we refuse to take the Lord's call as seriously and urgently as the Lord does. The Lord calls us now because he needs us now. Another turns to us now because she needs us now. We are summoned, like Moses, to release someone from bondage now. But we say "not yet"—while people stay in bondage and death. We go through the proper motions of involvement, anxious all the while that we are not prepared for it and accordingly stay safely aloof from that total involvement that ministry would require. From our own anxious perspective, we keep our fingers crossed, feeling "this one doesn't count." But how fearfully this one does count, for another and in the eyes of God. This occasion for ministry will not come again.

The unlikely carpenter from Nazareth read from the scripture of the release of the captive and dared to say, "This day the scripture is fulfilled." It is not *self*-confidence that breathes such claims of immediacy but an attunement to the movements of God and God's unlikely comings.

For "I will be with you" is a stern rebuke only because it is a faithful promise, a promise known by every man and woman who has ventured into the wilderness at God's bidding, not knowing where they were going.

"I stayed by the dying man, not knowing what to do, so I just held his hand. He opened his eyes and smiled and whispered 'Good-bye' and died."

"I walked the streets of the impossible neighborhood, my head hanging from the misery of not knowing what to do. Then a man stopped me and said, 'I want to talk to you, Reverend...'"

"When the fellow began talking to me on the plane I realized this was only a one-hour conversation. There weren't going to be any repercussions, pro or con, from whatever I did. I wasn't trying to get or keep anybody in the church. He didn't even know my name. Those things I usually fret about secretly didn't count on this one. So I wasn't trying hard to do the 'right' thing. I just tried to understand what he was trying to say. Imagine my surprise when he said at the end that this was the turning point of his life."

"When I saw the girl that night I was so tired I couldn't think of theology or ethics or counseling or anything else. I just said, 'Let's go someplace where we can relax.' So we went to the back of the bowling alley and I sat there with my shoes off (pretending I was changing into bowling shoes). I don't really know what we talked about. I think I probably talked about myself as much as she did about herself. But when it was all over, it seemed the most real thing that happened to me that day."

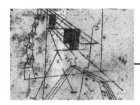

# 6

# Thirty-eight Years on the Verge

*Now in Jerusalem by the Sheep Gate there is a pool, called in Hebrew Beth-zatha, which has five porticoes. In these lay many invalids—blind, lame, and paralyzed. One man was there who had been ill for thirty-eight years. When Jesus saw him lying there and knew that he had been there a long time, he said to him, "Do you want to be made well?" The sick man answered him, "Sir, I have no one to put me into the pool when the water is stirred up; and while I am making my way, someone else steps down ahead of me." Jesus said to him, "Stand up, take your mat and walk." At once the man was made well, and he took up his mat and began to walk.*

John 5:2–9

Only a few steps away, in the surging waters of the pool, there is healing, vitality, strength, a new life. But the man lies ill *beside* the pool, separated from health and restoration by only a few steps, but separated also, decisively and tragically, by his own resignation to what he thinks is his destiny: "Vitality is there, and I am here, and we are separated, perhaps trivially, but unbridgeably. I don't have the help I need to change things; and anyway, somebody else always beats me to it. My lot is to be here, on the verge, not there in the midst of vitality. Other people are in the swim, but I must watch from the edges."

Jesus' answer seems to be something like this: While you are waiting and watching and ruing the distance between yourself and immersion into the creative and healing forces, while you may feel on the verge, you are really already fully in the midst of these forces. "Stand up, take your mat, and walk." When you feel most immobilized before urgent needs and expectations—a minister on the spot—exactly then and there you may be in the best position to make your move, to minister on the spot.

Thirty-eight years must be close to the average length of one's ministry. How many of those years are spent on the verge? How many of those years are spent waiting and watching, waiting for the extra help, the extra training, the extra experience, the right moment, the right circumstances which will immerse one fully in God's healing work? How much of a day, how much of a career is spent watching from a distance, perhaps great, perhaps tormentingly small, while others seem to be fully immersed in significant ministry? How many of those years are spent waiting with the rueful sense of separation between oneself and the significant currents of events in God's world?

In the Halloween preparations in our home some years ago, the oldest attempted to initiate the youngest with talk of terror, of witches and goblins that roamed abroad in the dark. But the youngest was undaunted, "If *I'm* there, they won't be real." This remark may be 10 percent bravado, but it's at least 90 percent self-deprecation. "If I'm there, they won't be real." There may well be such magnificent and splendid and terrible goings on. But never while I'm around. Such things never happen to me. Down deep, I know I'm only a kid, playing at this.

Most of us most of the time divide the world into two parts. On the one hand, there is the real and the significant and the vital; on the other hand there are our own affairs. There is the field of action, and there are the sidelines where we sit, perhaps as confirmed spectators, more likely as bench-warmers, waiting for action. In newspapers, in novels and films, in history and biography, we see significant events proceeding with appropriate signs and wonders; we see meaning proclaimed; we see purposes articulated. This is the appeal of drama and literature, history and biography: The significance of significant events is made clear to us. Astronaut and detective, physician and scientist charm us and attract our envy with their self-confident participation. They know what they're doing, and what they're doing seems to us especially real and potent. But we remain the readers and the spectators; it can't happen here. We turn our backs on the author or artist who dares to claim attention for the humdrum of ordinary lives such as ours without delineated significance. "Is not this the carpenter…here with us?" "Unless you see signs and wonders you will not believe."

The significant events of the world—and of God's dealing with it— move with signs and wonders. God's revelation, God's grace, God's judgment, God's call—these things happen to people with an impact and with a flourish, with dramatic preparation and confirmation, with events recorded and significance delineated. So each of us feels. As for me, we each tell ourselves, I hear about them in orderly and dramatic fashion from professors and books. There are notable and exciting and effective ministries in my time, and I can read of them. God may even be moving decisively with people down the hall or down the street, and this too I can observe. But for my own affairs, I am not part of any of this, not really and not yet. The daily affairs of my ministry are at least as unlikely raw material for significant involvement in God's work as the people of Nazareth found this carpenter's life. Although perhaps I am only a few steps from the pool, I am still not in it.

I know all about the dramatic possibilities of personal counseling, and I watch with fascination the reports of others who venture into this pool ahead of me and can report, in their case studies, some of the wonders of such intimate involvement and significant changes. But when the high school girl stops me in the hall on Sunday evening with her half-disguised, badly articulated sense of personal difficulty, this isn't the same thing, or not the "real thing." It's not the time, it's not the place, it's not the way this dramatically effective counseling can go on. She's not able to articulate her problems clearly, to develop insight, to achieve rapport in the way that counselees in the case studies are. Most significantly, however, I'm just not ready. She ought to be able to see that I'm only wearing a kind of mask. I don't yet have the experience or the resources that make me the kind of minister she needs to bring God's healing. So, encounter with her is not a moment for immersion into the pool. She is to be dealt with kindly, perhaps desperately, perhaps helpfully, but without the conviction that this encounter is really a moment of the genuine and significant ministry that God intends and that I am waiting and watching for.

79

I know all the theories of the moods and rhythms of worship, how God reaches down and we reach up and meet with a spark of re-creation. But worship in the seminary—that was for hearing what professors or other students had to say or else something to contend about. And worship in my church—that is something to plan with the deacons about, to fret about late Saturday night, to spar with the organist about, to conduct with or without some pleasure and some confidence on Sunday morning. But it's always on the verge. That God should reach down and speak a radical and direct and personal word to me in the midst of Sunday morning worship—this is as remote and unlikely as the sick man ever getting into the pool. I—like him—know too well all the reasons it can't happen.

The full and responsible participation of my congregation in the community and world around them—this takes a sophisticated theological and sociological understanding of the issues, and this takes a concern and dedication, signs and wonders, that I and these people don't now have. Maybe sometime after this congregation grows into maturity, or maybe sometime in another congregation—maybe sometime I can get out of this carpenter's shop and into an effective ministry.

Some can testify to a clear conviction of God's vocation for them, an unshakable confidence that God has called them, and a sure knowledge of what God has called them to. And there may even have been moments in which each of us has momentarily experienced such conviction. But for the most part, we are still looking and searching—looking to find that clear sense of leading that can become the foundation for effective ministry. "I have no man to put me into the pool…I am just involved in my ordinary, undramatic groping and fumbling."

Most difficult and impossible of all is that acceptance of God and that faith in God's acceptance that we talk so much about and that we have known momentarily from time to time. We are on the verge of this personal faith constantly, so close to it that we are experts in it. But that we should actually experience it, here and now in this hectic, transitional, mixed-up, humdrum kind of life that we now lead—what could be so fanciful as that idea? Someday the sense of God's presence and call will be clear and convincing to us, but not yet.

Meanwhile, while we try to fill the many large and sometimes mysterious responsibilities of the ministry, we may feel more like a boy wearing his father's clothes, or imitating his father's voice on the telephone and hoping no one will notice; or a girl scolding her dolls in an exasperated maternal voice, disguising her own longing to be held and rocked to sleep.

Or as ministers trying to comprehend and engage the forces within and between persons, within the church, and within the society that the church must confront, we may sometimes feel like the small boy looking through the knothole of a fence while the big boys are smoking, or playing football, or talking about girls. Or maybe we are like the small boy who has brazenly climbed the fence and is trying to keep up with the big boys at their exploits. The small boy lives with feelings mixed between fear at having his brazenness and weakness uncovered and in the buoyant hope of eventually really deserving a place inside the fence among the big boys. Or maybe we are like the small girl who has persuaded her mother to make her older sister take her to the movies with her friends, knowing that the price of inclusion will be the demand that she fetch the sodas and popcorn.

Or perhaps we sometimes feel more like the young adolescent, head over book, or walking home alone, overhearing the other girls tell of their exploits from last Saturday night or their plans for the next. "Someday maybe I, too, will be in, but now I wait on the outside, looking in and looking on." Or like the adolescent boy when he does date, who feels it as a time of learning how to get along with girls, of getting ready to have the kind of good times other people seem to be having naturally.

Or maybe, going through all the motions of ministry, we feel like a member of a college debating team or the student government. We earnestly, maybe even feverishly, spend ourselves as in the debating and the politicking, maybe even win acclaim and success. But deep down we know all along that we are not engaged with the "real world." We are practicing, developing skills, getting ready, waiting and watching for the "real" engagement that is to come. Thus, we may describe our careers with analogies of adolescence. Perhaps for many of us, they are more than analogies; perhaps they are also history.

However long one's ministry has been, ten days, ten months, ten years, one may still feel like one who moves into a new house or a new office and looks around making note of things *with respect to the future.* "That chair will be comfortable to sit in as soon as I finish this paperwork that keeps me in the desk chair now. That window will be pleasant to read by when I start spending more time reading. That wall will be a good one for the two pictures I have in the attic. The neighbor seems pleasant; I'm going to enjoy getting acquainted with him." But all these experiences remain as future anticipations. We are still making these promises to ourselves until the day we move out. They never come to pass. So, too, with our anticipation of finding the clear word to speak, the steady discipline of time and mind, the patient calmness of personal empathy, the vital engagement of others' ardors and responsibilities.

81

Our sense of being on the sidelines, of being not yet engaged in the "real thing," always has this expectation of imminence along with it. We are not in the pool yet, but we are on the verge. All it takes now is someone to carry us into the pool. Next time may be it. Just a little more preparation and planning, just a slight change in the condition and circumstances, then all will be well. We each have our own way of promising ourselves that moments of significance, of faithfulness, of effectiveness are just ahead: Right now the circumstances aren't quite right; I'm too unprepared, too ordinary, too fumbling. Just a little more patching here and a little more polishing there, then I'll be in ministry. Then I'll be ready to say, "Come down, Lord." I'll just get my New Testament Greek a little better. I'll just get a little better acquainted in town. I'll just lay a little more foundation with the deacons. I'll just wait until the family isn't quite so demanding. I'll just wait until I can figure out a little better why some of these people hang back. I'll just wait until we get the budget up to where we can support a good program. I'll "begin" just as soon as I can have an assistant or some layperson to help me with some of this busy work. If the "real thing" can't happen here, it will happen just around the corner. If I'm not really active and engaged in it—well, I almost am. Carry me down into the pool, and I'll be healed. That's the kind of help the ill man and we look for.

But that is not how he was restored. *There is no such thing as being on the verge.* It only feels that way. Either be sick where you are, or else there, *where you are,* "Stand up, take your mat and walk." There is no moratorium possible. There is no exemption assigned. Wherever you are, however you are, you are living as fully in the world, you are exercising as complete a ministry as you ever will. People are looking to you now (and perhaps away again), affected one way or another by what you say and do. And they won't come back again whenever you finally announce that you are "ready." For you never will. Our moments come and go, and our actions and decisions in them, even in the most unlikely moments and the most unprepared states, affect us and others irrevocably.

For we are assured of two things. First, the future, the next stage and the next moment to which we may look with so much confidence, will turn out to be just as murky as our present state. That moment—getting married, raising the budget, getting to know the deacons, getting the children out of diapers—which we expect to provide the purifying baptism will instead only bring us new murkiness. It won't really change anything. We—who are not prepared for the Lord and his call now and know we are not—will never be prepared. That final purifying baptism in the pool is not to be ours.

Significant events never happen with the clarity and dramatic preparation that they come in retrospect to have in the writing of history and biography. What seems in the novel and the drama, in the history and the biography to be of such lucid significance, happens, if it happens at all, only in the midst of the most humdrum and ordinary and unlikely and unprepared moments. Only in retrospect do events yield their pattern and their significance.

For, secondly, we are assured that this present hectic, ordinary, unprepared life is not really ordinary and is not really unprepared. For God is here. We don't have to send pleadingly, "Come down, Lord." God is already here and working healing to us and through us. We don't have to beg or wait or yearn for special baptism in the Beth-zatha pool. We have only to rise up *on the verge*:

*"Stand up, take your mat and walk."*

God does not call us *out* of our life as we know it into ministry, but calls us to find our ministry *in* our life. We needn't despair of present humdrumness, hindrance, or hecticness. Nor must we hide in false hopes of the future, of another place or time where signs and wonders and certainty and readiness will abound. It is just possible that in the unlikeliness of your present situation and with all the unlikeliness of yourself as you now are, even in the routines of your life this day—not even waiting until your headache feels better or until you get those letters written, or until you get those phone calls made or until you get away from the phone, or until you have a chance to look up something in the reference book, or until you can consult about it or even make up your own mind—God may touch you to cleanse, to reveal, to chasten, to claim you and your ministry.

# 7

# Joseph: Frozen Power

So we struggle through barriers of our own making that separate us from ministry by holding up faithlessly high expectations for our own readiness and also for the readiness of circumstances to accept our ministry. Yet there are barriers, too, erected by others' faithlessly high expectations of us—assignments that freeze us out of ministry, by elevating us and isolating us and muting us. They sideline us from engagement with the human predicament and God's hopes for it—or seem to. Joseph, that ardent caregiver whose story is told in the opening chapters of the New Testament, is archetypal for this dilemma.

It was said about him that he was "a man who always did what was right." A model citizen, a man whose retirement tribute or Chamber of Commerce award or obituary could have written itself, as though the life had been lived just for the tribute—the tribute scripting the life, not vice versa. A model citizen, the kind the neighbors gasp to the reporters about after a violent outburst or an elopement to South America, "He was the last man we expected to do something like *that*!" He was a man who always did what was right.

In every Christmas manger scene, every Christmas pageant, one figure stands tall, central, and unnoticed—Joseph, the father who is not the father. Just as in your household and mine, baby and mother, animals and visitors all get more attention than the sturdy, quiet figure in the center of the action. Joseph is an apt symbol for the role generally accorded ministers: prominent, dutiful, robust, yet shadowy and marginal, never quite looked at directly. "What exactly is his part in the story?" That's how it is every Christmas in the manger scene. That's how it is all year around for most of us. That's how it was for the first Joseph in the Christmas story, absolutely dutiful, crucially dutiful, yet kept in the shadows.

The story starts out with Joseph at the center; he has the leading role in the first chapter of the New Testament, in the first chapter of Matthew. Joseph is at the center, but look how the story goes:

Now the birth of Jesus the Messiah took place in this way. When his mother Mary had been engaged to Joseph, but before they lived together, she was found to be with child from the Holy Spirit. Her husband Joseph, being a righteous man and unwilling to expose her to public disgrace, planned to dismiss her quietly. But just when he had resolved to do this, an angel of the Lord appeared to him in a dream and said, "Joseph, son of David, do not be afraid to take Mary as your wife, for the child conceived in her is from the Holy Spirit. She will bear a son, and you are to name him Jesus, for he will save his people from their sins."…When Joseph awoke from sleep, he did as the angel of the Lord commanded him; he took her as his wife, but had no marital relations with her until she had borne a son; and he named him Jesus. (Mt. 1:18–21, 24–25)

No matter what happened, Joseph stayed tough. When his fiancée turned up pregnant, he may have been dismayed and humiliated, but no one knew it. He always did what was right. If he was hurt or angry, no one knew it; he stayed in control—in control of himself, in control of the situation. Denied his bride, shunted aside from fatherhood, if he felt wronged, he covered that pain with his own righteousness. Good Scout ever, he would make no trouble, just put her away privately, the decent thing, you know.

Of course, when he was told to do otherwise, he changed his plan and did as he was told, still tough, still righteous. When he discovered that the higher right, the still more self-sacrificing right, was to give Mary a home and to give the baby a name, then, of course, that is what he did—and no sex! If he felt used, abused, or cheated about having a marriage in name only, about being a father who was not a father, no one knew it. Doing the right thing was more important than finding personal satisfaction. He provided for the baby, scrupulously, relentlessly— the second chapter makes clear just how much out of his way he went on behalf of the baby—just as he was told to do.

That is all we know about him: He always did what was right.

I learned to play Joseph, quite literally, the year I became a teenager. Miss Gardener and Miss Swearer, who produced the Christmas pageant that year, cast me in the lead role, and they taught me how to do it just right. Though their script was only one of many in a boy's life, not even the first, not even the most rigid, it was a clean and spare script, for being up front in the church.

First, they enticed me with promises: a big part, an important role, top billing, right next to Mary. I said I would do it. Joseph had exchanged promises, too; Mary would become his wife and bear his children. Then, like his, my expectations were shattered. The script turned out quite different from the billing and the built-up expectations different in the same way. Once recruited and on stage, my instructions were simple and absolute: don't move!

Eyes down, one hand benignly on Mary's shoulder, the other hand out in an open receptive gesture, welcoming all pilgrims, I was to freeze, stock-still, the only person in the pageant unmoving and unmoved, the lead role become part of the scenery. I was the centerpiece, even the altarpiece of all the action, yet totally removed from the action, a figure-head. Presiding, in charge but uncharged, steadfastly going through the motions without moving a muscle.

Going through the motions of standing still: Miss Gardener's and Miss Swearer's script for me was Matthew's script, scripture's script, for Joseph and the most common script for the minister, learning to run in place. We must strike a decisive posture without moving, without effecting anything or affecting anyone, thoroughly domesticated, leashed, mute.

When ministers believe the promise of top billing, the invitation to be the center of the action, but don't understand that the script requires them to freeze—when they misperceive the promises as the script—then they spend many heartbreaking and ulcer-plagued years trying to make a difference, trying to have impact and effect, trying to leave the world different from the way they found it. Spent, burned, and burnt out, at last they discover what the Miss Gardeners and Miss Swearers knew all along, that the script only requires them to freeze, to simulate action, to be a prop and scenery for others to act out their pageantry.

When a minister looks up in twinges of pain and anger from these fruitless efforts, the Miss Gardeners and Miss Swearers watch blankly, truly dumbfounded and perplexed, appalled not at their own unresponsiveness but at the minister's feverishness. "We thought you understood the script. All you're supposed to do is stand still and be the centerpiece."

Suppose I had taken Miss Gardener and Miss Swearer literally when they said "Be the hero." Suppose I had been busy playing Joseph as I conceived him: concerned husband, tender father, generous host, thoughtful sage. I might have fussed about the manger, urged Mary to take a nap while I kept the vigil, graciously received visitors and their gifts with flourishes and with speeches. Suppose I had moved into the role and about the stage with such vigor? Suppose I had played Joseph as I thought I had been invited to? Suppose I had played Joseph as I most wanted to? Suppose I had played Joseph in the way that felt most authentic?

If I had tried to be a vigorous, genuine Joseph, then I would have encountered what any minister encounters when he or she ventures into authenticity and integrity of call. I would have encountered what sociologists call "role conflict" and disruption of the system.

Wise men, shepherds, and Mary would have been confused and balky. Instead of matching my spontaneity with their own, all action would have come to a chaotic standstill. My own version of Joseph as God's appointed one would have been an obstacle to their playing out their own scripts, instead of an invitation to leave their scripts and to become authentic wise men, shepherds, and mother. The audience would have been offended and dismayed; a real living Joseph is not what is expected. Miss Gardener and Miss Swearer would have dissolved in fury (expressed in typical code of course: one would simply have said, "Well…!" with the other standing close behind, hands on hips). An unscripted, spontaneous, expressive Joseph, especially an emotional Joseph, was not wanted, is not wanted. I was not wanted, at least not unscripted.

"Freeze!" the police say to the robber caught in the act.

Any minister who has ever followed the script, or even accepted casting—that is, every minister—has discovered that the casters and the scriptwriters don't mean it, at least not in the way one thought they did, at least not consistently, at least not as something to live your life by, at least not with your having the power to carry through. Seducers never do mean it as earnestly as the seduced suppose.

For me, as a thirteen-year-old Joseph, the abrupt discovery, the unveiling of the script, came promptly and therefore almost painlessly: "Leading man?" they said, "Forget the busy hosting and benign solicitude. Just freeze!" I didn't have time to take the role of leading man seriously and bustle about the stage acting out this role to which I had been recruited and was commited, before being chagrined and stranded with the countermand "Freeze!" I have seldom been as lucky since. Few are. Far more often, we have been energetically preoccupied in midstage greeting shepherds, rocking the baby, performing whatever other chores we have been assigned, content to be doing "what was right," secretly savoring the admiration and merit we believe we are earning, when suddenly the houselights go up, and a voice booms out, "Cut! What are you doing? You were just supposed to freeze!"

The abrupt discovery came late and painfully for my grandfather, one who most decidedly and most admirably "always did what was right," as a faithful and imaginative minister/husband/father. He endured a seven-year engagement while his bride-to-be cared for an aging mother. He laboriously gardened huge plots every summer to reduce his claim on church budgets, frequently no more than $1,000 per year.

Already successful as minister in a large city church in his thirties, he relinquished that when his denomination asked him to move West at the turn of the century to start a new church. Once he had moved, the denomination abandoned its support, leaving him stranded and a failure. Now off the career ladder, stigmatized, shunted aside by church officials guilty over their own miscalculation, he was unable for years to find another church, and then never one able to fully require or appreciate his talents. He never complained, persisting faithfully and creatively at whatever he was assigned. Never complained, that is, until late in his life, when the houselights suddenly came up on the psalms he had been reading for most of his life, and he noticed that they were true, that the wicked had prospered and that he hadn't. Aging and semi-invalid, he showed me the newspaper accounts of American Legionnaires cavorting at conventions, thriving while flouting every line of the script he had bound himself to and which still bound him. Bitterness escaped from him in the form of his warning to me: "Take a good look down the road before you make any big decisions."

Why can't mentors pass on this hard-won wisdom—or at least wink when they pass on the role assignments—this wisdom that the roles of ministers are isolated roles, not part of a genuinely working ecology, that the people supposed to play those complementary roles that are needed to justify the scripts of ministry aren't doing so. Fathers can't warn or wink, because the rules forbid such confession of feeling duped or angry, because that is to confess loss of control.

There may be gender differences in ministers' response to the scripts of going-through-the-motions chores. Cinderella is a woman's story, the dream of escape from the chores, once the hero comes along and makes the slipper fit. Women can dream of escape from the chores, because they know that life is more than the chores. For men, the chores faithfully performed *are* life. Women, hardly to their advantage, *can* imagine and sometimes wait for the rescuer, the prince to awaken them with a kiss, the fairy godmother to brandish a wand, the hunter to slay the wolf, the wonderful wizard of Oz to take them home. Indeed, women assign these roles to their men, to no one's advantage. But men cannot depend on such a savior (any more than be one, for the women), only on their own efforts—fully as futile as waiting for Prince Charming. It is not from their chores that men seek a saving. Men may seek rescue from loneliness and meaninglessness (and cast women as rescuers), but not from their chores. For men, chores are the solution, not the problem. Chores are to be pursued, pursued even to the breaking point.

The biblical Aaron is known now mostly for how he ended up, faithless manufacturer of an idol, the infamous golden calf, that so angered his scriptwriters, God and Moses, that they destroyed it. But when this episode is read within the whole story (Ex. 4—7; 32), we see how Aaron was seduced into this fateful deed by venturing to do a good deed. He was only doing his best to follow the very script that they had set for him. They had commissioned him into a ministry of assuaging his people's plight, and they had taught him to use props at hand for miraculous effect (for example, "Say to Aaron, 'Take your staff and throw it down before Pharoah, and it will become a snake'" [Ex. 7:86]). So in Exodus 32 when the people were desperate and leaderless, when they felt abandoned by both God and Moses, when they needed drastic help, Aaron undertook an honest ministerial chore, a good deed, the best he knew. He took gold jewelry at hand and fashioned a golden calf—it looked strong and saving! And God and Moses said: You should have known better; even with all that responsibility, you were just supposed to freeze.

Oedipus is now known, thanks to Sophocles and Freud, as the villainous murderer of his father and seducer of his mother. But he was lured into such disaster precisely by playing the hero flawlessly, just as everyone wanted and for which they applauded. Volunteering exile from what he thought was his native land, in order to avoid causing disaster there, he went to Thebes and played hero as all scripts taught: He killed a threatening marauder, answered the riddles, saved the city, and married the queen. This impeccable record of noble intentions and heroic deeds was turned on its head by fate and Freud to make Oedipus—and the Oedipus in each of us—the villain and victim, a just man faithful to his duty and lured by it into disaster, when it turns out that the call to duty is a seducing lie.

The plight is not unknown to lay people aspiring to live out with zest and fidelity their calling to the Christian life. Doug Abbott, a man well known to me, has lived his call with a vigor and a skill and an effectiveness that deserve praise (and get a lot from some people), but earn only fearful disapproval from his wife, who wants a faithful chore boy, a "good boy," frozen in place.

Provide for, give of yourself to your family, your church, your community. These are the calls Doug has obeyed, precisely and unswervingly. Providing for the family has meant working hard and taking risks. It has meant starting his own business, building his own factory on the edge of town, trying new products. Every move has resulted in more comfort and more security for his family; the changes have also meant, in this case, more time with his family and a happier disposition. But every move he has made has been resolutely opposed by his wife as a threat to the family security. She has attacked him as reckless and uncaring, as deliberately risking his family's welfare for crazy new ideas. His wife, fearful and unhappy, has mobilized neighborhood support, and Doug now lives with the reputation of being foolhardy and selfish—a reputation he has earned precisely by being careful and selfless.

When his church sponsored Cambodian refugees, he quietly offered some jobs in his factory and just as quietly refurbished one of the buildings on the property in back of his factory for housing. Deserving praise, he got more accusations: You're taking a chance hiring so many of them—suppose it turns into charity? Why can't you let the others in the church carry their share?

Doug is Don Quixote, spurned for taking the impossible dream seriously. He is Oedipus, made the villain and the scapegoat for the ills of the city, for undertaking no more and no less than his city wanted. On the whole, Doug is warmly liked. It is only his overcommitment, as people see it, his unabashed seriousness and energy in pursuing the role he was taught—that is what offends the community. Somewhere, Doug has missed or has ignored the fundamental message: freeze. But they will have their way with him and subdue his spirit. Lacking appreciation and instead villainized, in late middle age he is gradually subsiding. "Let them do it their way. Let them make their own mistakes." He is gradually surrendering. They will have their way with him, and their way is: freeze. It's another word for "burnout."

Employ a man as leader, whether as president or as a school principal, whether as new Kiwanis president or Boy Scout leader, and there is much rhetoric from others about high expectations for new accomplishments. But the real expectation is: Don't rock the boat. Most ministers get the message well and play out this dream effectively, meeting both expectations at once, appearing to move while standing still; the appearance of being a leader while frozen. Promotions and plaudits abound for the minister who plays well enough to make others feel energized and led while no one has to move. Everybody knows that except the intrepid good Scout Joseph, taking expectations and promises more seriously than they were meant, building castles doomed to crumble.

## The Freezing Power of Frozen Power

Though the Joseph script blunts and mutes natural spiritual energies and plants one isolated on a pedestal, the script does—unfortunately—generate its own kind of power. But it is a power to freeze others. Joseph does have center stage, and we easily enjoy exercising the power it offers. I got a charge out of presiding over the manger scene. The difference between bringing my own energy to the role and getting my energy from the role is the tragic predicament. But once Joseph lets his own power be turned off, frozen, he does feel a new power surging; unfortunately, it, too, since it derives from the freezing of the role, is frozen in its own way and freezes others. The frozen Joseph has a kind of Midas touch: Everything he touches must turn solid, too, to match his frozenness, an agent of Miss Gardener's and Miss Swearer's freezing touch.

"You were commanding," they said afterwards. "You looked in charge, running things." At the cast party "Mary" stood off by herself, giving me long wide-eyed looks, preteen adoration. And for weeks afterwards, kids who had played kings and shepherds would pass me in hallways with eyes averted, a vestige of the deference they had shown me in the pageant. For, as dutifully, even abjectly, as I may have complied with the script, the script called for me to be magisterial. Though I gave up playing Joseph my way, their Joseph played me. Their Joseph dominated me, but in such a way that others perceived me as dominating them. I may have been frozen, impotent, but I was frozen in a pose of power. I may have felt a puppet, I may have *been* a puppet, but I was a puppet who pulled the strings of others. They didn't say, "You froze well," though I did, and though it was important to them and to me that I did. They said, "You were commanding." The role became real. Overruled, I became ruler.

To become Joseph is to change the axis of orientation from horizontal to vertical. Give up the outward reach (to peers, to frontiers) for a more secure upward grasp. Give up action onstage for approval backstage. Lest abandon bring abandonment, give up abandon for a bonding with the powers, opting for the risks of bondage over the risks of abandonment. Give up being "a real boy" for being a "good boy." The Joseph deal, the Pinocchio deal.

For that is what we risk in occupying the Joseph role as ministers. We comply with the script for the payoff. To avoid all the ignominy and scorn that it would have cost to be my own Joseph, I complied with being Miss Gardener's and Miss Swearer's Joseph. Led man rather than leading man. But it still felt like being on top, on high. I had an in on high. My status was now derived, not self-defined, but it was still status. I was making the deals all teacher's pets make: give up spontaneity, its delights and its risks, and get the security of sponsorship, the comfort of patronage. Give up the risks of excess for the privilege of access. To authorities. And the power that brings.

## Victim and Victimizer Are One

Ministers are often and readily portrayed as victims of stereotyping and role-typing. The principal purpose of this chapter so far has been to draw that very portrait. Ministers are just as often and just as readily portrayed as perpetrators of stereotyping and role-typing, forcing people into postures and roles to fit their own schemes. The remaining pages of this chapter propose to show that these two portraits, stereotyped and stereotyper, pushed and pusher, are one portrait. These pages will try to make it clear and plausible that the minister, frozen in place, fixed, stereotyped, role-typed, once one comes to fill the role, to play the script, must support that role by enlisting others in the same script.

The key is in the artificial, manufactured nature of the role; the role is not necessarily fragile or precarious, but it is artificial. The imposed role has not evolved; it has been constructed. It is not part of an ecological balance—or perhaps it is an archaic survivor from the balance of another era—so that it is not in a natural give-and-take relationship with the environment around it. It is constructed and imposed on, inserted into, the environment—more like rape than embrace—so that the minister is forced to construct an environment to match the role.

If the minister is puppeteer, shoving a fist inside other people's lives to manage their doings, then he or she is also a puppet, compelled to just such doings, such managing, by fists shoved inside his or her life. Sometimes, in a fine, if constricted, symbiotic balance, the hand maneuvering you, the puppet, is the hand of the puppet you are maneuvering—the self-sustaining, self-defeating arrangement of many a married couple, many a professional and client, many a parent and child, many a politician and voter—mutually paired idols all, mutually dependent (not interdependent), mutually freezing.

When I was Joseph, a thirteen-year-old Joseph learning to be a lifetime Joseph, Miss Gardener's and Miss Swearer's Joseph, I was definitely not employing method acting. I was not told to get into the spirit of being Joseph, then let my inner promptings, my inner prompter, take over. That may have been what I wanted, what I had first thought I had been promised; but I was not allowed that. I was told what to do, and all attention was on my doings, Miss Gardener's and Miss Swearer's attention and energy, therefore my attention and energy, and therefore the attention of my fellow players and of the audience. This was not less true because my doings were so constricted, but more true. If what I had to do was to freeze, to stay fixed in place, then my doings were all the more important to everyone. "Be sure to keep your eyes on the manger and not look around!" they said. "Keep your eyes there, don't move!" I recited to myself all during the performance. "How still you stood!" everybody said admiringly, quite different from a remark such as "You were really Joseph," to which I might have aspired and earned had Miss Gardener and Miss Swearer—and hence, I—been part of a different Christmas message. To be Joseph was to be defined by these assigned doings, no more and no less.

Later, people would say to me and other Josephs: "How tidy you keep your lawn," and "Your voice sounds so good from the pulpit," and "You have such a nice smile and broad shoulders," and "You tell jokes well," and—a more insidiously freezing role casting—"You are so sensitive." Narrow doings all. Me. Feeding such comments and fed by them, Joseph redoubles his energy on lawn care, voice projection, body building, joke telling, and sensitivity—if this is who Joseph is, then this is how he must try harder to be somebody—in a way that inevitably enlists others in this project. Children must dig up weeds—they need the discipline and the exercise; it's good for them. "Keep Off" signs go up. "Do Not Interrupt" signs are strictly enforced when I am working at voice practice. People must be smiled at and they must smile back at jokes or people must expose their vulnerabilities so Joseph can "do sensitivity."

A frozen Joseph, limited to a narrow task, limits and shapes how other people can relate to him. People in the pageant had to adjust their roles to mine: I wasn't going to adjust to them. They had to come to where I was and kneel reverently, because my posture demanded it. They had to let their eyes go where mine did, not meeting mine. They had to handle their gifts themselves; I stayed aloof, above such transactions. My doings shaped theirs. My fixedness limited them, shaped them.

If I was learning to be Matthew's Joseph, as well as Miss Gardener's and Miss Swearer's Joseph, then I was learning how relentlessly and insistently Joseph would play his role and sweep others into the action. Take Mary as my wife? Certainly! So Matthew 1:24 seems to say. Abstain from sex? Firmly! Escape to Egypt? Immediately! "Joseph got up, took the child and his mother by night, and went to Egypt" (Mt. 2:14). Joseph will play his part in Mary's script and Jesus' script when he has to, and he will do it determinedly. But when his time comes to take the lead, then they will play their parts in his script, their supporting roles, and they *will* do it. "Right away, Mary. I have the travel orders. No time for breakfast or laundry or saying goodbye. We're going now."

Suppose in my eighth-grade pageant, on the crowded stage, one of the shepherds trips on his unfamiliarly long robe and falls toward me. My natural impulse is to put out a hand to catch him and to ward him off, so he doesn't bump me or Mary. But Miss Gardener's and Miss Swearer's Joseph is frozen—"Don't move"—and in obedience to that lofty posture I must withhold my hand, let the shepherd fall. But when he does bang against me, knock me out of my pose, Miss Gardener and Miss Swearer or not, I reflexively throw up a hand, which is now too late to help but strikes him alongside his head. The hand that would help while protecting is frozen into a hand that can only defend and hurt. To be Joseph is to be trapped into this defensive belligerence, so that it seems to become inevitable even when it doesn't come naturally.

## To Be Joseph or Not To Be

To be Joseph is to want to wear to school a brightly striped sweater, your sister's, because you feel good and look good in it, but then to think of the jeers it would get on the bus, then to put on the usual jean jacket and mix with the crowd at the bus stop, ready to be the first to jeer at any striped sweater.

To be Joseph is to impulsively compliment a woman on her new hair style, just because you like it, only to have her pull back haughtily as though you had made a pass, then to resolve to henceforth withhold any such friendly gestures and to remain strictly "professional." Or else— really only another version of frozen power, another constricted and safely emotion-free pattern—to accept the assignment in her response and to fall into the habit of making flirtatious wisecracks, suggestive remarks, and innuendos: "Long lunch hour today?" "I can see why your blouse popped a button, and I am glad." It's easier, really, a more smoothly predictable pattern, to treat each other just as sex objects, a familiar script you can both follow, no unnerving surprises.

To be Joseph is to say to a lover or a daughter or a wife, "You seem tense and upset today," offering sympathy and support and caring, only to have her shoot back, "You can be so critical sometimes." So—especially after a succession of such episodes wears down your warmth—you pull back into a properly masculine stony silence or else begin to return the fire, gradually growing into the judgmental role in which she has cast you, casting her as victim of the constant critic she has cast you as. Instead of risking warmth, risking rejection, it turns out, somehow, to be easier to play along with this script; at least you know where you are, and at least you have some place in her life. As judge you are somebody she knows how to deal with. As object of scrutiny and correction she is somebody you know how to deal with.

To be Joseph is to be a five-year-old walking with your mother in a strange part of town looking for a toy store that had advertised special bargains in the paper and, after she says, "I wonder where it is," you impulsively run over to some men to ask where the toy store is, and she is embarrassed and scolds you, "Don't bother them like that." Chagrined, compliant, and proud, you grow up to be a man who is self-reliant, a man who will study the road map by flashlight, drive around blocks and blocks, never pull into a gas station to ask directions, curse the incompetence of the highway engineers, and snap at the passenger who makes a suggestion.

To be Joseph is to rush to hug your son after he falls while climbing up on a wobbly chair, only to have the hug interrupted by a voice—over your shoulder or in your head?—"Warn, teach, don't coddle, be firm, don't pamper, be strict," so you pull away and scold, "That's what happens when you climb up places you're not supposed to be." That somehow feels right. The voice is stilled, and you've done what you should have done, in spite of the wistful tug for the aborted hug.

To be Joseph, frozen and outwardly unmoved, is to be the fifty-year-old man, immaculately dressed, dominating a class reunion dinner. He has just been dismissed from a significant publicly visible position. Not visibly bitter, not defensive, not recriminatory, he is analyzing, in detail and adroitly, the sociological and political and institutional processes that have made this decision inevitable. He is holding a kind of seminar on institutional decision-making—it all might have happened to somebody he had heard of once a century ago and a thousand miles away. Only his insistence on imposing this seminar on the dinner party suggests that something personal is at stake, but not a tremor shows in his voice, not a hint of pain or anger. He is a Joseph who "always did what was right." He stayed in control, in control of himself by keeping control of the situation: He dominates the conversation (lest someone offer sympathy?) and he is master of the institutional processes (lest the whole thing seem too personal?).

To be Joseph is to be outraged over a piece of political skullduggery in your town and to prepare a memo that says so, only to remember that your outrage will offend many, so you mute the outrage with a more "balanced" analysis and a retreat into abstract principles. You eventually discover after several such episodes that you enjoy the feeling of an undivided community, and that you savor compliments such as "He certainly keeps people together"; you savor them so well that you begin to inflict "peacemaking" on others and to rebuke "troublemakers," those who get agitated about injustice at work.

To be Joseph is to be a teacher recognizing with awe the growth of a class—as steady and as lovely as watching a flower bloom in time-lapse photography—thrilled at the mounting discoveries, the deepening risks the students take, the questions and theories they venture, the building of trust and bonds, the increasingly muscular skills they display in analyzing problems, and their increasingly loftier imagination in dealing with them; and to be equally awestruck and thrilled and grateful at your own capacity for intervening at just the right point to keep it rolling—to permit yourself a brief glow of satisfaction—"This is what you are called to do and what you do well"—only to have one frustrated student whine, "We've wasted an hour going around in circles instead of asking the teacher to get us straightened out." Momentarily intimidated and easily regressing to a more familiar pattern, they fall silent, and you become talkative, begin to play the new/traditional role assigned by this student. You make a lucid analysis of the problem they have been discussing, the alternative solutions, and the reasons for choosing one solution over the others. To your simultaneous delight and consternation, the rest of the day and even in bed that night, what you remember with relish and a tingle is your vigorous analysis, your decisiveness, and the enthusiasm the class showed afterward. So, despite yourself, you open the next session with a speech. "Let me help you get started by laying out the questions today."

To be Joseph is to venture to preach with an energy and a passion and a directness that derives from your conviction that there is something in the Bible text that you desperately want your people to hear. You look them right in the eyes while speaking intimately to them from your heart, not from a manuscript. It feels like real communication, not a performance. But they parry your invitation to spiritual passion with remarks such as "I guess you didn't have time to write a real sermon this week." So you revert to performing, without passion, being more aware again of their eyes on you rather than your eyes probing theirs.

To be Joseph is (1) to yearn for the richness and color and depth of life that you know is your natural birthright and a God-given promise; (2) to be assigned, instead, a task, a fixed role; (3) to adopt that task as yours, that role as you, and to devise ways of sustaining it, to the point of (a) enlisting others into the script implied by your role and assigning them their corresponding tasks and fixed roles, and (b) bringing vigor and energy and imagination into protecting those roles, theirs and yours, from the erosions and ravages of that rich birthright of life, once—and still?—your treasured promise.

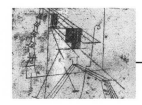

# 8

# Confessions of the Golden Calf

*So all the people took off the gold rings from their ears, and brought them to Aaron. He took the gold from them, formed it in a mold, and cast an image of a calf; and they said, "These are your gods, O Israel, who brought you up out of the land of Egypt!" As soon as he came near the camp and saw the calf and the dancing, Moses' anger burned hot. He took the calf that they had made, burned it with fire, ground it to powder, scattered it on the water, and made the Israelites drink it.*

Exodus 32:3–4, 19–20

I never wanted to be a golden calf, yours or anybody's. I was content to adorn you as earrings, to jingle when you danced, to glisten with sweat as you labored through the day, to be admired sometimes, and, at those times when you found other adornment, to be quietly stored away. I was content to be a part of your life, an important part, but only a part. I never wanted to be your golden calf. I never wanted to be the center of your life, the focus of your most intense and most suppressed emotions, the one you danced around, the one you sweated for. I wanted to be close to you, not set apart, not cast and frozen, not pedestaled, not altared, not altered, neutered in pretense of endowing potency. I never wanted to be the one to whom you attributed your saving, your past and your future. Why did you say I had brought you out of captivity? You had brought me.

Why did you expect me to be the answer to your prayers, to show you the way you had lost, to fill your loneliness, to rescue you from the wilderness? How did you expect me to find you, to guide you, to be intimate and potent with you, when you stripped me from yourself, when you molded me into something I am not, gave me face and form that you needed but that are not mine, when you set me apart and lifted me above you?

I never promised any of the things you expected from me. I never threatened any of the things you feared from me. I didn't want you to believe I was endowed with these grand powers, because the belief was so destructive. How could we live together that way, with you expecting so much from me that I could not deliver, with me wanting to relate to you in an intimate way that was forfeited by your recasting of me?

I never wanted to be the excuse for your frenzy, for your fears, for your fantasies. I never wanted to be the object of those frenzies or fears or fantasies, only to be with you in them. I didn't want to be set up as lording over you. I didn't want to draw fire for making grand promises any more than to draw fire for failing to keep them. Inert as I was in your life, willingly inert, suspended, hanging, even dangling, given motion only by your movement, even as I did nothing to raise myself up, any more than I could raise you up, so I could not bring about my own destruction, any more than I could bring on yours. Most decidedly I did not want to be flung into the fire and ground into powdered oblivion, to be swallowed. I only wanted to adorn, to be admired occasionally, to be sometimes joined with you. This final joining now violently imposed upon us is intimate indeed, but so destructive to us both. If only you had left me dangling as sometime adornment, and had not cast me as your savior. I did not want to be your golden calf.

When I visited you in the hospital, I, too, was scared by your disease, and by all the busy people and machinery, and by wondering what we could talk about. But we did talk—and you did most of it—about these fears, about your hopes and your memories and your disappointments. You opened up and let me share so much of your life, past, present, and future. I talked, too, sharing in more openness than most people ever find. It was an intimacy that both of us craved and treasured; we said so. That afternoon at the hospital promised something new in each of our lives, a lasting intimacy that would build on that precious breakthrough by your bed. That's what we said.

But something else happened. Was it because you were lying down and I was sitting up? Was it because such intimacy was so unfamiliar and unpracticed and more than a little fearsome? When we next met, for a drink, it seemed you didn't want to continue the intimacy but to avoid it. In fact, you even seemed to want to avoid me. You no longer saw me as the partner in intimacy that I wanted to be and that I thought I was. Now you saw me as a power—the power, I guess, of one who knew so much about you and knew how to know more—a power to be coveted and a power to be feared. You had invited me close and then fended me off. You invited me to meet you, to talk of love and hate and fear and hopes and disappointments. But when I arrived, you—we—spoke of politics and neighbors and baseball. You stuck to safe topics in order not to offend me and maybe also not to tempt me to use the powers of our more intimate knowing.

I worked hard at your committee meetings. I took them seriously, and I wanted you to take me seriously, but not as intensely seriously as you did. I threw myself into the committee work. I did my homework. I followed the discussions closely. I analyzed the issues deftly for you, and I proposed solutions that were well thought out and imaginative, solutions that reconciled differences adroitly and that you adopted enthusiastically. These offerings were to establish myself as member in good standing of the committee. I wanted to be one of you. Instead, they set me apart, or you set me apart. You set me apart with a great deal of ambivalence. You admired the energy and skill with which I worked. You even came to depend on them and on me—"Let's wait and see what he comes up with." There was a special attentiveness when I spoke. But you also came to disapprove, to avoid, to dislike, and maybe to fear my energy and my skill and your dependence on them. You caucused without me. You clustered at the other end of the table. The hush when I spoke was exaggerated, like a protective blanketing, paying tribute to my words but also isolating them from the rest of your discussion. Sometimes I thought you paid more attention to whether I was frowning or smiling, intense or flustered, than to the analyses and arguments that I was so earnestly attending to. You would say "You are always right" with appreciation and admiration, and with impatience and irritation. You welcomed it when I advanced the discussion, but you also felt judged and inadequate. When you murmured together cynically and wearily about the committee work and dropped the occasional acid remark about the tediousness and futility of it, you wouldn't let me join you, like the teacher's pet at recess on the playground. Somehow I became the champion or custodian or conscience of the committee and all it symbolized. You felt better about yourself and about the committee because I worked so hard at the business and so you needed me and catered to me. You identified me with the structures and with the demands and with the nuisances of the committee. You treated me the way we have always treated ministers, set them apart as embodiments of the powers or the obligations we feel are necessary parts of our lives, but from which we feel alienated: We admire the ministers for playing this role but also find or make them strange and estranged.

My very desire, and the intensity of that desire, to be involved and close, a real part of the committee, and my effectiveness in doing that, made you make me remote and special.

101

I never wanted to be your savior, only your minister. I wanted to join with you, the congregation, in a covenant of search and trust in which we might together come closer to finding the sure roots and the clear directions for our lives. I needed that, and so did you. I had some gifts to bring to that covenant and that search, and so did you. I wanted to be your minister, not your God. I wanted to join with you in the search to find and trust and obey our God.

But you seemed to think that I was already on God's side. You seemed to treat me as someone who had already found God, securely and fully, as someone who lived the holy life, who could answer all the hard questions, could guarantee God's presence and good will, and if I would, could guarantee your salvation, someone who pronounced the judgment of God on your life. When I came close to join you in search, you backed away and measured a distance between us, with your formality and deference and awkwardness, just as though I wore a dazzling halo or a damning scowl. I wanted to be your partner and you made me your parent.

We in the congregation never wanted to be the ones to make good your vocation as minister and your spiritual pilgrimage. We never wanted to be the ones whose conduct and belief would be the means of vaulting you into heaven or dropping you into hell. We never wanted that power over you. We never wanted to be the ones you would look to so anxiously, constantly taking our temperature to see if our faith and biblical sensitivity and social responsibility and ecclesiastical loyalty was hot enough to fuel yours, rich enough to nurture yours. We never wanted you so dependent on us that our slightest stumbling out of step with you became interpreted as abandonment of the faith and of you. We never wanted you to need us. We needed you, but we didn't want you to need us to need you.

God, I never wanted to be the place where you lodged, the place where you lodged your trust, your vision, your expectation that people can be free and healthy and loving. Couldn't you stay away and on high, as God is supposed to do, let us negotiate at a distance, and maybe even let me sometimes hide? I never wanted to be one that you counted on to be one of your adult people. It's easier to be a child, but you never seem content with that. I never wanted to be taken that seriously, that relentlessly. You don't let go. It is as though you *need* me, as though you have so much commitment to me and investment in me that it makes a crucial difference to you how I respond, how I behave. I never wanted to be taken that seriously, to be trusted that much, to be burdened with that unswerving love. It is almost like unmerited adoration. I feel as though I stand awkwardly on a pedestal, high and lifted up. You seem to mean it. But I am restless and wary. It feels like a setup for a fall, it feels like making me a visible target, it feels like mocking me. But when I try to climb down into the depths where I belong, you say it doesn't feel that way to you, and you keep lifting me up. I never wanted you to rely on me, to believe in me, to invest in me, to treat me as though I had power, as though I were so important to you that all other facts were less important, to you and to me, than that fact.

When you reach toward me, it is so determinedly that I panic. You are so steady and firm in your reach that it makes me fear that you are punishing or judging me, crowding me, wanting to take something away. But you respond to my panic, to my testiness, to my unease, to my persistent resistance, with that same disturbing thereness. You are just looking at me, gently and steadily, waiting.

# PART THREE

---

**particular,** 1. of or belonging to a single, definite person, part, group, or thing; not general; distinct; peculiar to one. 2. specific. 3. out of the ordinary; unusual; noteworthy; special. 4. dealing with particulars; itemized; detailed. 5. not satisfied with anything considered inferior; exacting; extremely careful; fastidious; hard to please.

# The Particularity
# of Ministry

# 9

# Administration *vs.* Ministry

Administrative work is the bane of ministry, by most accounts. As ministers often see it, it is the unwelcome and unmanageable burden they carry that retards the progress of their ministry as they want to pursue it. Ministers report themselves caught in administrative work when they want to be in ministry. When ministers are asked what part of their work they most enjoy or think most important, they mention pastoral activities or preaching or teaching first, and administration comes last. But when they are asked how they actually spend their time, administration comes a clear first, and the others lag behind. This is the often-replicated finding of research studies. The dilemma becomes more poignant and more urgent when we hear individual ministers tell of their despair: "I wanted to develop a meaningful program and close pastoral relations. And I could have. But we all got bogged down in the machinery of the church. Like quicksand, it just sucks you in. You can't help yourself." Or when we see ministers leaving the administratively burdened parish for what seem to be purer (i.e., administration-free) forms of ministry in teaching, in hospital chaplaincy, or in such secularized forms as psychotherapist, social worker, or politician. Or when we see the restiveness elevated and rationalized as an elaborate critique of the institutionalized structures because they blur vision, drain talent, and inhibit ministry.

## Two Kinds of Tasks

The conflict between administration and the purposes of ministry is most often expressed as a competition for time, effort, and energy between two kinds of tasks: A minister feels led by call, training, personal preferences, the expectations of seminary mentors, and the assessment of the needs of the people to invest in pastoral, preaching, or teaching activities. A minister wants to do those things that will advance the people's Christian growth, make them more forcefully to know the assurances and demands of God. But once actually on the job, the new minister feels compelled to invest heavily in administrative activities: recruiting, organizing, chairing, deciding, planning, arranging. At telephone, at computer, over coffee, in office, in study, and in living room, one is doing all the things required to initiate and maintain activities and organization, and not performing ministry.

What prompts this attention to administrative tasks is not always clear. The minister often reports it as deriving from outside demands: from the expectations of superiors, or of various constituents in the congregation, or from the autonomous requirements of the institution itself, an institution that somehow seems a necessary but not entirely integrated adjunct to the ministry one would pursue.

But it is also possible that the impetus to administration comes from within. It simply may be inherent in the minister's prime objectives. (Even pastoral counseling interviews and Bible study groups and evangelism have to be scheduled.) Or there may be something inherently (though unconsciously) attractive about these administrative tasks themselves, perhaps because they are more easily defined and provide more obvious evidence of achievement, perhaps because they provide relieving surcease from the more demanding tasks.

In any case, whether the so-called role conflict is between the minister and others or is within the minister, it is usually defined as a conflict between two different kinds of tasks, administrative *vs.* ministry.

## Two Styles of Ministry

But even though they talk about the conflict in terms of time and effort, they may often mean more than that. It may be that ministers experience the conflict more keenly and more deeply, not merely as a conflict between two different kinds of tasks, but as a conflict between two different ways of doing the same tasks.

*Administering* vs. *pastoring*. A minister who lists pastoral activity as first choice among his possible roles may be ready to tell us—if he were given a different kind of questionnaire that permitted him to do so—that he wants to have a kind of pastoral attitude and approach about all his ministry. He wants to be a pastor, whatever he may be doing. He may mean he wants to approach all his personal relationships and each of his various activities with a freedom and a joy, an acceptance and a concern for others in which he finds a particularly effective expression of the gospel, a particularly effective ministry. A minister may find it especially easy to express this ministry in relatively formal situations of counseling, but to be a pastor may mean to express this attitude with one's parish and one's parishioners in whatever activity.

But this minister feels this pastoral stance contradicted by an administrative stance that he unwillingly and unintentionally finds himself drawn into. This conflict between two different styles of functioning saps away his sense of vocational integrity and personal fulfillment. Instead of being concerned about persons for *their* sake, and instead of putting himself in *their* service, he finds himself treating them in relation to *his* purposes and *his* institution's. The I-Thou relation he intends becomes contradicted by the I-It relation he finds himself pursuing. Instead of entering into their lives and ministering to their troubles, he finds himself asking them to enter into his concerns (as promoter and guardian of the institution) and to help to solve his problems. Instead of expressing trust and freedom, he shows himself fretful, concerned for results, and calculating how to achieve them. Instead of evidencing the faith and confidence in healing resources available to all others from outside of themselves, he finds himself trusting himself, his own diagnosis, analysis, prescription, manipulation. Instead of being free and open, he is calculating and controlling.

How can he be two things to the same people? How can he be two kinds of person himself? How can he plan successfully to recruit a Sunday school teacher at the same time he tries to be open and helpful toward the needs and plights of her life? When she reports the plights in her life as part of the reason for declining the Sunday school class, what does a minister then respond to, her needs or the Sunday school's? How does he develop his relationship with her, with what ends in view and with what style—as an administrator and salesman, or as a pastor and healer? He can hardly be both things to her.

How can he be permissive and understanding toward the natural expressions of the teenagers in his church, at the same time that he is responsibly aware of the "organizational problems" occasioned by the footprints they leave on the wall of the room that the women's society has just redecorated?

How can he lead his deacons to understand the freedom and grace of the gospel in the devotional part of their monthly meeting and later worry with them about the procedures of the communion service or urge them to more conscientious parish calling?

Even scheduling the next session with a counselee requires an attention to detail and conscientious and skillful problem-solving that may violate precisely the spirit of freedom one tries to create within the counseling session: "Well, if you find that your baby-sitter can't be there at 2:45, call me, and I'll see if I can change my 4:00 appointment to 3:00. But I won't be able to let you know until about noon that day, because the 4:00 person is out of town until that morning. If that won't work, I'll try to come out to your house, so that you won't need a baby-sitter, if I can finish the luncheon meeting early enough so that I can get out to your house, and we can have a good talk, and I can still get back to the church by 4:00."

A pastor is a shepherd but the image is ambiguous. Is a shepherd one who risks life itself to find the one lost lamb? Or is the shepherd the one who, with dog and staff, herds the sheep along the path already chosen for them to follow?

Pope John XXIII explicitly announced the "pastor" as the controlling image of his reign. The shepherd is a prominent image in the New Testament writings bearing the name he chose. But look what John XXIII did to the administrative structure. His pastoral pontificate had to be followed by an administrator, who made the preservation of the institution his keynote. We can have the two in sequence, but apparently—as any pastor knows—not simultaneously and in the same person.

*Administering* vs. *arousing to mission.* Another minister might put her prime goals differently but find them equally contradicted by the pressures to be an administrator. Rather than being pastor, she might most of all want to lead her people to the vision and to the willingness and freedom to extend their own self-investment into broader circles of need and life. She wants the affairs of the city and of the world to agitate them fully as much as the lunch-hour schedule in their children's school, the redecoration of their own home, or a successful fair at the church. Whether in the pulpit or committee meeting, in personal counseling or at a church dinner, her purpose is to enlarge her people's understanding of who they are and what they are expected to be. But how can she do these things when she is unavoidably the responsible administrative head of the quite local institution, the church? As with the pastor impeded by administration, the question is the same for this woman: How can she be two things to the same people? How can she be two kinds of person herself? How can she be a symbol for the expansion of self and concern, when she is unmistakably the symbol for the local neighborhood institution, which necessarily constricts investment of self.

How can she try to recruit a prospective Sunday school teacher with the argument or with the assumption that the education of the church's children has high priority at the same time that she wants to upset just such prevailing priorities held by this woman and others and expand their sensitivity to the needs of persons far beyond the confines of the parish. The dilemma is all the keener when she has chosen this prospective teacher precisely because this woman does have some sense of mission, which the minister wants her to communicate to the children.

How can she organize a meeting to expand people's concern for housing needs in the city, when the very act of organizing the meeting and recruiting attendance inevitably implies a narrowing of focus on the importance of this meeting in this place—a claim symbolized by the fact that the minister is investing herself in the "administrative" chores of arranging this meeting herself rather than, in fact, in the broader mission she was directed toward.

And—the near-cliché dilemma—how can she, by word or deed, try to stretch her people's vision without risking loss of their hearing, loss of their participation on the occasion when she can reach them, and loss of their support of the position from which she would speak and act? How can she minister to them without losing the opportunity to minister to them, except by careful and tedious administrative fence-building? How can she justify accommodating herself and her ministry to this need for fence-building, on their terms, without sacrificing too large a portion of that call to mission, which is the purpose of the whole thing?

## Choose Which Master

If administration and ministry contradict each other, then one must go. If the terms of the dilemma are those expressed above, then the prospects of "holding the two in productive tension" or any other compromise seem doomed. The more plausible solution would seem a forthright choice. We see this choice made on every hand.

Some pastors choose administration. They choose to devote their efforts to administrative tasks, and they choose to "be" administrators in every role. In pastoral contacts they respond to personal need and personal difficulty with a calculating, diagnostic, action-oriented approach. They promote mission through administrative and political finesse, managing budgets, manipulating the right people into strategic positions. Most of us deplore this choice of administration over ministry. Perhaps we deplore it for good reasons: We may believe that pastoral and mission goals are hardly met unless persons' insights are deepened and expanded through more profound encounters than the administrative style permits. But we may often deplore the choice for administration on more primitive, prejudiced grounds: We are perhaps fundamentally suspicious of the kind of task and style that administration is, the routine, humdrum manipulation of the things and people of the world. We are predisposed to think that such fare simply is not exalted, not magnificent enough to be allied with the purposes of the ministry as we see them.

Therefore the choice is more often made the other way. The dead weight of administration is sloughed off, and pure ministry emerges. If it is the denominational tie that is blamed for the administration, then this is ruptured and a freer context sought. If it is the local church institution that is to be blamed, then this is to be forsaken. Pure pastoral ministry can be sought in a hospital chaplaincy and pure mission in the city redevelopment agency. Or even if the administrative tasks are retained, the administrative style can be renounced. Administrative tasks can be approached with a pastoral style. The administrative problems can be essentially ignored and become instead the occasion for establishing rapport and for exposing deeper levels of personality and personal relationship.

But perhaps the problems of administration need not and ought not be put in terms of such a sharp polarity and disparity from other ministry. And perhaps the fact that the problem is so often put in terms of such polarity is another clue to the dilemma the minister experiences.

## Administration: Stereotype and Scapegoat?

Ministers' antagonism to administration is often curiously extreme and vigorous, often with a relentless, heedless passion that would be called, if it were applied to a social group, a prejudice. The organizing, recruiting, planning, arranging, troubleshooting, and problem-solving activities of the minister are too seldom viewed rationally or carefully, to discover which are constructive and which are wasteful; instead they are most often lumped together under a single label—administration— with which they can be sneered at, dismissed, and blamed for failures of ministry. Whatever the large or small failure of ministry, administration is most often blamed. Whether in the privacy of one's own brooding over less-than-ideal pastoral relationships, whether in the Monday luncheon group of ministers sharing frustration over failure to arouse people to a vigorous sense of mission, whether the frustration is escalated into an elaborate, highly rationalized critique of the structural facts of church life, these organizing, structuring activities are by far the most popular target. One is tempted to paraphrase Tertullian's account of the scapegoat persecution of the Christians: "They take the Christians to be the cause of every disaster to the state, of every misfortune to the people. If the Tiber reaches the wall, if the Nile does not reach the fields, if the sky does not move, or if the earth does, if there is a famine, or if there is a plague, the cry is at once: 'The Christians to the lions.'"

Whenever books are unread, families estranged, sermons uninspiring, people not aroused to mission, laity not elevated to the theological literacy, the cry is always the same: "Send the administrative work to an assistant." Yet such scapegoating, such solution by segregation, always exposes the irrational prejudice that lies behind it. For getting rid of the alleged devil doesn't solve the problem that it was blamed for. Disposing of the administrative tasks doesn't provide remedy for the deficiencies of ministry for which they are blamed. On the contrary, the facts seem to be that when administrative tasks are disposed of by redefining roles and restructuring organizations, by hiring secretaries and assistants, by abandoning organization, new impediments arise to take their place, and these, too, usually get branded "administrative." The solutions, whether reorganization or larger staff, tend to breed their own new and inevitably "administrative" demands. And each minister must finally face that moment of truth when he or she does succeed in carving out a morning or a month absolutely free of administrative demands or distractions. One discovers, far more often than not, that one's aspirations, for ministry or for study, or for writing, remain unfulfilled and still victim of distractions; and for the responsibility for this, one must look inward. More elaborate reforms in structure or changes in career intended to abolish or to obviate administrative drain on ministry far more often than not prove equally illusory: house-churches, redevelopment agencies, hospital chaplaincies, merged parishes, hardly turn out to require less attention to organizational life and somehow still don't bring in an age of pure ministry.

The preceding section has put the problem of administration as ministers put it, as a contradiction of ministry. I have explored this way of putting it as vigorously as possible to see how much truth there is to such analysis. There is some. But—I now want to contend—there is not enough validity to this argument to warrant the frequency with which it is offered and the ease with which it is accepted. I now think the preceding is something approximating the rationalization of a prejudice. Segregation is our favorite solution: keep those inferior, debilitating elements where they belong and away from the purity of ministry.

In the last section of this chapter, I shall propose equality and integration. I shall claim that the elements of administration—in narthex conversation, in committee meeting, in telephone call, in writing agenda and memos—are vital encounters and valid occasions for creative ministry, even though they look a little different on the surface. I shall contend that these administrative encounters deserve full-status membership among the occasions for ministry, on full equality with preaching, counseling, or mission outreach. In fact, full integration is necessary or the other forms of ministry are impoverished. Administrative encounters provide a uniquely vital occasion for the fashioning of ministry—be it pastoral, arousal to mission, or whatever—because they are occasions of immediate involvement in which minister and parishioner share a problem together.

Such will be my argument for equality and integration. But I expect as much resistance to such proposals among my minister readers as they are dismayed to find among their parishioners in opposition to proposals for social and racial integration or same-sex marriages. In each case, it seems to me, the resistance is primarily involuntary: Administrative work somehow just doesn't "feel" as right or as good or as important. Administration turns us off.

When we do admit administration into the household of ministry, it is usually as a second-class servant, a kind of nanny or houseboy role, welcomed because it is necessary to sustain the high-status roles, perhaps even beloved, so long as its inferior status is kept clear. My suggestions later in this chapter, intending full integration and equal status, will be misunderstood by some as arguing for a servant-like supporting role for administration.

These then—if I have portrayed accurately in this section a common feeling about administration—are signs of prejudice. Can administration occasion dynamic give and take between persons, significant enlargement of ideas and purposes in people's lives, the gradual molding and fashioning of Christian ministry? No! (Can any good come out of Nazareth?) (Everyone knows what people from that section of town are like!) (Everyone knows the threat those perverts pose for decent society!). In these activities the minister feels trapped in the unworthy bustle on the edge of the Beth-zatha pool, and the only way to get where the healing action is—where pure ministry is—is to be picked up out of this hubbub and put into the pool. To try to say to him "take up your mat and walk," "where you are, in the midst of this busy confusion and without need to escape it into the pool, minister"—such a suggestion is alien and intolerable.

## One Source of Prejudice: Mistrust of Self

If a minister's reactions to administrative work are exaggerated and unrealistic in some ways such as those described above and labeled "prejudice"—or to the degree that they are, or when they are—this raises a question. What is it that "prejudices" a minister against administrative tasks? What provokes a minister to turn against them with exaggerated vengeance? I would put forward an interpretation that may apply to some ministers some of the time. It can be stated simply: Perhaps ministers devalue administration because that *is* what they do and do well.

Perhaps the best starting point for this discussion is to turn around the question that is most often asked about the dilemma. When researchers discover that ministers value least exactly what they spend most time at (i.e., administration), the question most often asked is: *Why do they spend so much time doing what they value least?* This kind of question is what leads to strategies for reducing the amount of time spent in administration—strategies that generally turn out futilely. (Something in the minister and/or the job seem to promote administrative work, whatever tactics are taken to avoid it.) But suppose we ask the question the other way: *Why do ministers value least what they spend most time at?* What if we supposed that the minister, in his or her *behavior*, perhaps intuitively, is responding to the valid call to ministry that is in administrative work (or more generally, is deriving some important professional or personal satisfaction from it)? Then the question becomes something more like: Why, in one's evaluation, does one turn against oneself and what one is doing? Why repudiate what one spends two-fifths of one's time doing?

Is this a prime instance of the mistrust we feel about our circumstances and ourselves? When we get restive with these administrative activities and keep saying that we want to discard them so that we can get on with real ministry, how often are we mostly saying, "If I am doing it, it cannot be very important or effective." Or, "Whatever activities and circumstances I am now concerned with cannot be the best there is. There must be people and situations and encounters still awaiting me that are more likely occasions for ministry than anything I am involved with now."

Objectively viewed, these administrative tasks might be important and effective instances of ministry. But we are barred from making that objective assessment by the fact of our own involvement. Our own participation (and perhaps satisfaction) brings down the judgment of unworthiness. A common epithet for expressing this disparagement is "administration."

The application of this epithet sometimes visibly escalates. Activities that seem to transcend "administration" and move into "ministry" themselves still get dubbed "administration." First it may be recruiting people and arranging for room and chairs for a discussion meeting on community housing that seems irksome. Then it may be having to sit with a human relations council steering committee to set an agenda for a community-wide meeting. And even when one is engaged in the actual task of finding housing or people or when one moves to positions of considerable power and influence—on the city council or leading the church into building low-cost cooperative housing or fashioning national denominational policies—there is still the temptation to feel that one is still on the verge, tending machinery, while the important action lies just beyond. The pool recedes as one advances. What we once fantasize as the next step, which will put us into the swim, leaves us once we take it, still feeling on the verge. We often label this newly discounted activity "administration."

Or first we may discredit the tedious "administrative" work of collecting book orders for a study group or of arranging personal borrowing privileges at the nearby college library while we long for "real" theological discussion or study. But then keeping the group or one's own study disciplined and on the topic seems to require routine "administrative" tactics of a sort that still seem to separate one from the heart of the study. But even immersed in the study, teasing out meaning seems to demand routines of collating, note-taking, cross-referencing, and

115

analyzing that still seem mechanical, in a sense even "administrative" and still tantalizingly remote from the "real" work.

There is another clue that our mistrust of administrative work may sometimes imply a mistrust of self. It seems to make a difference whether the administration is mostly an individual responsibility or is part of a large institutional structure. Administrative work on one's own shoulders is what most often becomes the irksome albatross. But administrative work that is a well-defined and sanctioned part of an institution often seems a lighter yoke, much more bearable, precisely perhaps because it is in harness with something. The pastor who leaves a parish because its administrative burdens seem so unbearably distracting from ministry may turn to the "purer" ministry of college or hospital chaplaincy and engage cheerfully, even unnoticingly, in a far greater proportion of committee-attending, memo-writing, and telephonic-tending of machinery. Pastors who find it most burdensome to keep the wheels turning in their church may find it an enjoyable relief to attend committee meetings of their council of churches or denominational structure or the board of visitors of their seminary or to engage in correspondence and other administrative activities related to these institutions. Our administrative drudgery often gains a validity and meaning from being part of a substantial institution that it doesn't enjoy so long as we are on our own.

Many of us are afflicted with a view of ourselves that makes it seem simply improbable that whatever we find ourselves doing can be significantly related to important goals. And we are afflicted with high standards and high aspirations that make it easy for us to measure our performance, whatever it is, as inadequate. It is much more consistent with our self-image to think of ourselves as still "on the verge," still in preparation and anticipation for the significant, "real" performance to come, still performing the administrative preliminaries and not the main event we want entered in the record book.

Perhaps what makes studying or preaching or counseling attractive and promising of significant accomplishment is that we are not doing it in large measure—yet! If we were to spend more time and self in these activities, the same reservations would creep in. We still can't fully invest ourselves, trust ourselves, expose ourselves in this particular encounter with city hall, this particular counselee, this particular reading or writing, this particular intensively prepared sermon series. These are still handled by temporary expedients, and we still long—many of us, much of the time—for the right occasion still to come when we will be ready and able, and the circumstances will be suitable. But so long as our ministry is functioning in large part in committees and conversations, in meetings and memoranda, it is these circumstances that we mistrust and devaluate and withhold ourselves from.

## Stand Up, Take Your Mat, and—*Minister!*

Caught in the disorderly hubbub of organizational chores, we need not gaze enviously at the nearby pool where there seems to be pure and vital ministry. The Lord comes and calls far more often where individuals are than where they look for him. When circumstances lead us into planning, organizing, troubleshooting, problem-solving kinds of activities and away from our preferred forms of ministry, perhaps they are to be respected, not disparaged, for doing so. Is ministry really to be found in neatly packaged roles, thirty minutes of preaching, fifty minutes of counseling, two hours of Bible study? These roles are abstractions, and they abstract minister and people out of life. Just because these are legitimate and useful abstractions, and because minister and people function in them comfortably, they are not thereby normative for all of ministry. When the purposes of church and ministry, the knotty structural demands and trivial annoyances of institutions, the ambiguous purposes, limited visions, earnest but feeble faithfulness, and downright perversity of minister and people—when all these get tangled up together in minor and major crises, this may be the occasion that demands the most creative and virile of ministry. Here is where a real issue confronts real people. Perhaps it is not as grand an issue as those one would like to preach about, but it happens to be an issue where people—who are seldom as grand as one aspires to deal with—are. It is in the administrative snarls where one is far more likely to find passions aroused, masks lowered, neat roles abandoned, stubborn resistances revealed, and glimmering aspirations bared.

117

"Recruiting" people to a series of study or "dialogue" meetings is the time of encountering the mixture of aspirations, antagonisms, misunderstandings, yearnings, and apprehensions toward a more faithful life (which the study group may symbolize) that marks the present stage of their religious pilgrimage. Once safely captive in the study group, the spiritual growing edge may be dulled by the group's abstract and well-prepared routines.

The moment of spiritual crisis for a counselee is not so likely to be in the course of counseling, where matters follow reasonably predictable and manageable patterns, as it is in the agonies of "pre-counseling," when one is trying to decide whether to risk trust and confession to the minister and the God the minister speaks for. These are the critical, trivial, administrative, living encounters in which the minister does or does not reach into another's life with an element of grace.

It may be that purposes and direction for a congregation or a group get formulated decisively in the preliminary gropings for personnel and leadership and agenda and schedules. The minister who prepares carefully for his formal presentation at the opening session may have long since set the stage decisively and imparted more of his vision and impetus in the informal, hurried, "administrative" conversations by which he invited people to join the group.

A minister might develop forceful homiletical techniques and preach on God's grace for a lifetime without saying as much as she does in the way she greets an interruption during preparation of one of these sermons, or in the "trust" she shows a pre-teenager in leaving a message for his parents rather than calling back, or the "acceptance" shown a harried man's reluctance to join the scout troop committee.

When a minister is drawn into responding to the needs of a situation, perhaps she should be much readier than she usually is to respect the situation and her response to it as valid and significant in its own terms. To try to categorize an event as "administrative" or as "pastoral" may help to mobilize prepared attitudes and response patterns to deal effectively with the situation. But it may also, in arousing these prepackaged attitudes and responses, run the risk of missing altogether the occasion for ministry that the raw experience presents. The immediate response with which she intuitively tries to interpret and cope with events—even though it may seem routine and unexalted—may deserve to be trusted as ministry, without having to "elevate" the moment into the preconceptions and prepared responses of a "role." That pool may not have as much to offer as you already have going for you.

Call and purpose of ministry must first have arisen for most of us in concrete situations. Our involvement and call may well have been obscured under such abstract considerations as deciding whether events are "pastoral" or "administrative." Responding again intuitively to an event in its own terms, without classifying it as "administrative" or not, may be a time of recapturing lost call and lost zest.

When a deacon is late for a deacons' meeting or has great difficulty in following the communion procedure, this may have an organizational meaning that might evoke the minister's special role as leader of an organization: The orderly activities are disrupted; the disruption may require some repair, for the sake of the general welfare and the purposes that the orderly activities serve. Such an event may also have a pastoral meaning: There may be some disruption in the man's personality or tension in his life that is interfering with his performance as a deacon and may invite pastoral attention and attempts at remedy. But there is a sense in which speculation about either such possibility is overlooking the more immediate and more obvious possibility. Right here and now, as *this* man participates in *this* communion service or *this* deacons' meeting, there may be something important happening in his life that accounts for this slight deflection in the smoothness of things and that is hinted at by the deflection. Disruptions, whether viewed as administrative problems or pastoral problems, occur for reasons, and these reasons may be much more immediate, much more pressing, much more urgent, much more meaningful, much more demanding of ministry than the organizational or personal difficulties they produce.

Why can't a deacon serve at the Lord's table with equanimity? What anger, fear, guilt, unworthiness, or other attitude before the Lord may be betrayed by this difficulty at his table? A minister doesn't have to escalate his response to the level of lay-training programs or liturgical reforms, or psychotherapy, or any other grand diagnosis and grand solution. The meaning of the event may be in the immediate confrontation. What is more, the purposes of ministry, which sometimes get expressed through administrative or through pastoral "roles," may be expressed more fully by abandoning or transcending these roles and attending to this immediate situation. What is required is not a new set of procedures or rules intended to get the deacon to the meeting on time or help him follow the service more smoothly. The minister doesn't have to retreat into such a formal "administrative" role. Nor is it required for the minister to start probing into the man's personal life and relations with his wife (even assuming that such personal upset may be relevant). That would be retreat into a "pastoral" role. Each of these might seem better defined and purer forms of ministry. But what if the minister can trust himself and the situation enough just to try to cope with it on its own terms, the kind of annoying troubleshooting, problem-solving activity he so easily resents as taking him from ministry (in its more abstract and purer forms)? What if he doesn't try to diagnose the difficulty into something he can minister to? What if he just discusses the problem with the deacon: "It's hard for you to get the hang of this."

Addressed directly, not stiltedly and ministerially, and with the kind of trust expressed that his "problem" may be important in whatever terms he experiences it, the deacon may be ready to look at the situation himself: "This is different from anything I'm used to doing." From here, his sense of the difference and his awe of the difference can be naturally explored; perhaps his sense of how remote his life is from God will be set alongside the communion's assurance to the contrary. Whatever the direction taken, the result might seem to be some combination of administrative and pastoral activity, but will probably seem to minister and deacon to be neither. It will seem to each just more like a "good talk we had," and that will be ministry.

When a prospective Sunday school teacher excuses herself by telling of the turmoil of her life, this leaves an organizational problem of staffing the Sunday school, and one has to face the dilemma of turning on or turning off the administratively persuasive manner. It also invites pastoral attention to these professed turmoils. But the most immediate and simplest and also the most significant question may be: Why is she telling me *these* things *now*? The instinctive, annoyed response (which you so carefully and ministerially suppress) may not be far from the

**119**

mark: Why drag all these personal matters into the simple question of teaching Sunday school? Why does she summon up these excuses in response to this invitation? What is the interaction between the prospect of teaching Sunday school and these difficulties in her life? Is teaching Sunday school so terrifying that she must resort to extreme excuses—and if so, why is it so terrifying? This is precisely a question for the minister and, in a sense, only for a minister—as distinguished from the administrative and pastoral questions, which, in a sense, the minister borrows from the executive or the psychotherapist. Does she see Sunday school teaching as demanding that she pose as a model Christian, which prompts her to set against this model the despair over her real life? Does Sunday school awaken memories of childhood experiences that she may somehow, secretly or otherwise, blame for her distresses? Could she be expressing, in this mild form, a kind of complaint: God doesn't deserve my service since God treats my life this way? The *immediate* and religiously most significant meaning the event has may be in terms of such interaction between this moment and the persistent themes of her own pilgrimage.

A minister carefully and persistently guides her church into an enlarged sense of mission. But she runs into snags. The missions committee asks the trustees to postpone repainting for one year and spend the money instead on an urgent emergency ghetto project. When the trustees, angered, refuse ("We can't be irresponsible about our own property on a whim"), the missions committee, equally angered, call for a church meeting to reform policies and procedures in controlling funds. ("Those trustees, who never even come to church, think it's their money instead of the church's.") The structure and the mission of the church are threatened, and the minister must spend much time in fence-building, reestablishing communication, listening to impassioned outpourings, arranging meetings, observing parliamentary procedures, revising bylaws. What a nuisance to be so grossly distracted from the ministry she was just getting well launched—the education of her people, through sermons, study groups, and service projects, into a fuller sense of mission. Now she must put all that off in favor of "administrative" troubleshooting and perhaps feel considerable bitterness about being let down by people who are supposed to act like Christians and don't.

Or is it possible that in this hectic politicking and patching she is, or can be, working much closer to the cutting edge between her people and their mission than she ever could in the ministry she now finds interrupted. "Well, just whose money is it? Let's talk about that!" Here is an issue that people are going to struggle with, fully involved, no holds barred. Perhaps they don't hear the overtones of stewardship in the minister's question, which she would like to address and assume. If they take the question in terms of petty bickering, well, that is where they are and what is going to mobilize passions and searchings (as "stewardship" never could). If in searching to justify their answer to the question, they turn to criteria ("We put that money on the altar for God, not for the trustees," or, "God may not have anyone to do the work if we don't keep God's body here on earth healthy"), these still may not sound much like the seminary discussion of church as community of faith. But they are approximations that never would have been reached if the minister had started with the seminary-like discussion and tried to induce her people into it. And because in the politicking her ministry is where *their* passions are, these approximations carry a commitment, a clarity, and a permanence (perhaps even as a foundation for future development) that ministers undistracted by such disruptions may well envy.

Others who will envy will be those ministers beset not by passionate opposition but by indifference. When concern for mission is met by suburban inertia, here is another barrier to ministry that sometimes seems to invite administrative tinkering—organizing committees, study groups, projects in the church, joining a denominational committee on mission, finding a job in a more auspicious context. These more formal administrative responses are indeed distractions from—perhaps retreat from—the ministry of mission. *Perhaps* they will pave the way successfully for effective ministry—take minister and people from the verge and into the pool. But probably they won't.

But what about a more simpleminded, more direct kind of tinkering with the problem. If indifference and inertia greet the minister, perhaps this is what is to be directly confronted and examined. Indifference and inertia may be one kind of passion. There may be significant action and meaning, after all, embedded in the fact of indifference. This *is* a response people make, perhaps for reasons that are important for the minister to attend to, perhaps crucially central to the purposes of ministry. What uncertainties of self, of faith, of others, what aspirations, what fears, what mixture of jumbled religious and personal gropings make it easiest for the person to confront claims to mission by turning them off? Why not find out by asking? Maybe not head-on provocatively, at first, until people are used to such ministry in naïve address to the thing at hand. The minister asks, casually, in a deacons' meeting, "I can get a rise out of the congregation if I preach on raising children, on the economy, on sex, on politics, on practically anything. But when I talk about our responsibilities in the city, nothing. No fight, no interest at all…Maybe I don't make myself clear."

"It *is* hard to know sometimes what you have in mind. These things aren't so close to us as our children, or the economy even." Here is clear recognition of estrangement. This is no small confession and raises important questions needing, and apparently open to, exploration. It is apparently a relatively small step, not too difficult to take, from identifying indifference to acknowledging estrangement. Here in the indifference is where the estrangement is lodged and evidenced and can be exposed. It would be a much longer step, one probably not often taken, from a sermon on estrangement to acknowledging estrangement.

"Just what is it you want us to do?" The indifference is converted into an obtuseness, inasmuch as the minister has made some concrete proposals. When the minister points *this* out, the obtuseness now invites further exploration, and in a few more steps, becomes identified as a certain degree of fear. "Well, I guess I'd rather not pay attention to those kinds of ideas." And the fear is now open to ministry.

The minister might labor mightily through the preaching role, first to bring people to church, then to develop text, phrases, illustrations, and delivery, then to organize a post-sermon discussion session—all to make her congregation feel the estrangement or fear she feels them to be caught in. Most ironically, a main objective in this program would be to overcome indifference. But chances are slight of getting past the indifference into involvement with the text and message and into intimate personal experience of estrangement or fear; and the minister's frustrations over indifference are likely to continue. "I have no one to put me into the pool" of genuine engagement with the lives of these people. Yet perhaps the very indifference defines the engagement to which the summons is warranted, "Stand up, take up your mat…"

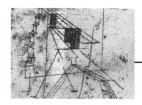

# 10

# Preaching as
# Risky Investment

Preaching is a function of ministry with compelling warrants in tradition and experience, perhaps the one with the clearest warrants of all. To be a minister is, among other things, or above all else, to be a preacher. To some, preaching is all there is to ministry. Yet preaching has gross deficiencies as an expression of ministry, and to invest oneself and one's ministry earnestly in the activity of preaching is so to constrict ministry (and self) as to distort it.

Some ministers may be so thoroughly and uncritically invested in the preaching role that they identify ministry with preaching, and thereby sacrifice ministry. Others may be so critically aware of the defects and limits of preaching that they stand aloof from the pulpit and thereby sacrifice ministry. Most ministers probably vacillate in the ambivalence, going through the motions of preaching, but half-heartedly, or with low depression—and thereby sacrifice ministry—because they know all too well that their preaching cannot do what it ought. We celebrate—and envy—those ministers who can freely throw themselves into a sermon, just as though it *were* the full and perfect word of God, and can just as freely stand back, with humor and contrition, and recognize how far short of communicating the Word of God the sermon has fallen and how much more ministry is still needed—for in the free, total investment of self in sermon, and in the free, total separation of self from sermon, there lie the greatest opportunities for ministry.

The same can be said of any other function of the ministry or any other institutional form of the church and its mission. Ministry and church do not exist apart from expression in particular activities and forms, yet expression in any particular activities and forms is to constrict and distort that which they would express. I bring up this dilemma not to prove it exists—that has already been amply done in the literature of our times. Nor do I intend to point the path to a happy resolution of the dilemma. I raise it rather to recognize the haunting predicament it poses for the minister and to lift up some of the characteristic responses to it.

## How Preaching Impedes Ministry

As a minister considers investing a significant amount of energy, time, and relationship with the people—that is, a significant amount of self—into the activity of preaching, its limitations haunt and discourage. For one thing, it *is* traditional, and its patterns *are* traditional, and it may be excruciatingly difficult for both preacher and hearers to break out of sleepy patterns to discover ways of communication that grip real issues for real people. Something about the pulpit, perhaps its very heritage and importance, stifles crispness, vitality, engagement, and spontaneity that may more readily emerge in other contexts, for example in a discussion group. Further, preaching is only one limited form of ministry, and to choose to maximize it is, intentionally or not, to choose to minimize other forms of ministry. This is true, of course, because time is limited; to really invest oneself in preaching is to commit much time and energy to this task, time that is thus unavailable for other tasks. But preaching may monopolize something even more important than time. It may come to control a minister's relationship with the people. The very act of preaching places a distance, severity, and uni-directionality in the relationship between the preacher and the preached-to, impairing other possible relationships. To be sure, some styles of preaching may mitigate this problem and some aspects of a minister's self may be revealed and known through preaching in a way that enhances other relationships. But self-investment in preaching may preclude and cut off other important relationships with some people. How can they "level" with someone—in business meeting or counseling or discussion group— who has so convincingly occupied the lofty height of the pulpit?

A prospective investor in preaching also faces two unavoidable facts that give pause before their combined recognition: One is the rich psychological satisfactions derived from preaching; the other is the scarcity of evidence that the preaching is having the objective effects one wishes. The walk from chancel to narthex after the sermon can be a disheartening moment, imposing a change in mood as abrupt and as icy as a sunbather's dunking in a cold lake. For there, in the narthex, you must stoke the burning involvement and sense of triumph felt from the morning's sermon and prepare for the casual nonchalance or the tangential enthusiasms or the gushy sentiment that greets you—and the sermon. This weekly reaction must raise nearly disastrous doubts about the validity of such investment in the preaching.

As the prospective investor in preaching you will also face the *particular* limitations of your own preaching. The preaching will demand more than you can offer: insight into the faith, and personal commitment to it, empathy with the people, facility at communication. You will also sense—deeply, persistently—the unreadiness of your own people to hear the word preached in the images of the Bible and the vocabulary of faith with which you know how to communicate.

These are some of the defects of preaching. Are these reasons for not preaching or at least not investing yourself in preaching, for going through the motions but without hope or commitment or vision? But do not the same limitations apply—the partialness, the ineffectiveness, the unreadiness, the tainted self-satisfying motivations, the impediments of tradition (or the over-enthusiasms of faddishness)—wherever a minister may turn to find true expression of ministry, whether in teaching, counseling, direct social action, discussion groups, administration, political involvement, and under whatever guiding image—enabler, pastoral director, shepherd, crisis repairer, or whatever?

What is a minister to do in the face of such ambiguity? Do you immerse yourself heedlessly and so fervently into your preaching (or other form) that you can overlook these limitations? Or do you preserve your integrity and testify to your loyalty to the values that transcend the forms by withholding yourself from a vigorous commitment to the preaching role? Are you most concerned to protect yourself from irrelevance or irresponsibility by getting fully and actively involved, in preaching or some other role? Or are you most concerned to protect yourself from idolatry by a cool, half-hearted participation in preaching (or other forms) so as to testify that you don't "believe in" these forms, but only in what transcends them? Or is there another way of participating: fully, not halfheartedly; yet responsibly, not recklessly? Can one "believe in" preaching—accept it as a fully valid and worthy form—yet not "believe in" preaching—not put religious trust in preaching to save?

Can you throw yourself into the role or the institution that is your particular chosen form of ministry, fully aware that it is only a particular and imperfect expression of that ministry, yet not be inhibited by that awareness from committing yourself totally and enthusiastically to it? Can you prepare and preach sermons with total discipline and wholehearted verve and without a regretful reservation, just as though this preaching were about to bring in the kingdom; yet, at the same time, can you be so unregretfully aware that your preaching is not about to bring in the kingdom that you are willing and able to recognize all the signs that may come your way that you need to modify your preaching or even give it up in favor of the greater claims of another role? Can you thoroughly abandon yourself and your qualms in the unreserved service of preaching at the same time that you are prepared, when need be, to abandon this same preaching? Can you let yourself go to preaching without becoming so enslaved to it that you cannot let it go when need be? This is freedom of investment.

Such freedom can be contradicted in two ways. One is slavish addiction to the partial. The other is slavish devotion to the ultimate. The first treats the partial—in this case the preaching—as though it were the ultimate toward which it points and as though it were deserving ultimate and absolute commitment. This contradiction to freedom seeks justification, righteousness, and fulfillment in terms of the discernible and readily verified good works and in terms of fidelity to specific obligations. This is the needful addiction against which Paul and Luther most leaned in their hymns to Christian freedom. The other contradiction to freedom is in the fearful inhibition to investment and commitment, which refuses to recognize the degree to which the ultimate is in the particular and holds out for that which can never be, the pure expression of the ultimate.

## The Bondage of Overinvestment in Particulars

There is a kind of bondage to preaching—as to any other role or form of ministry—that is a self-investment so thorough that it is more than investment and becomes self-identification. Preaching becomes important not as *an* expression of ministry and of self but as *the* expression of ministry and self. Techniques of exegesis and of voice, of construction and of delivery, effects in the pulpit and on people become not only cultivated and mastered, they become relied on—exclusively—as the means and as the evidence of faithfulness in vocation. Because the minister and ministry find their center, their justification, indeed the basis for their being in the activity of preaching—rather than in the fuller apprehension of ministry that preaching partly expresses and to which it points—this activity must be unquestionably served and defended as though *it* were the saving faith—which, in fact, it *is* for such persons. Competing claims on time and energy must be firmly set aside. Evidence of the need for other forms of ministry must be steadfastly overlooked. Signs that preaching—one's own in particular—is not having the effect one "believes in" must be resolutely denied.

The preaching role by which one feels justified must itself be justified by extension into and domination of all roles and relationships. Since one is not a minister who preaches, a Christian who preaches, a man or woman who preaches, but *is* a preacher, this must be clearly affirmed to self and to others at every opportunity. So that when one seeks the minister for personal counsel, is visited in the hospital, sits alongside him in committee meeting or worship, one is aware in tone and theme that here is the preacher. Such a minister is not free to minister—or in the long run even to preach—because he or she is in bondage to preaching, a bondage fashioned of exclusive reliance on it for definition and justification of self and of vocation.

There are ministers who similarly are in bondage to techniques and styles of personal counseling, administrative chores, one or another forms of direct social action, denominational committee structures, small group leadership, and so forth. Or perhaps the truer picture for most ministers is one of multiple and shifting bondages.

This is a kind of *hot* bondage, to be distinguished from the *cool* bondage (to be described next) that avoids any investment and refuses to identify ministry with any particular form or activity. On the face of it, one seems about as different from the other as manic exuberance differs from depressive withdrawal. But the bondage is the same, because in neither instance is the minister (like either the manic or the depressive patient) free to pursue ministry as circumstances and calling may require. The two forms of bondage may be similarly rooted (just as the manic's overlust for life and the depressive's withdrawal from life may both be rooted in a profound absence of self-esteem): Both forms of bondage may be the most satisfactory expressions of vocation a minister can make in the absence of a convincing confidence that self and vocation are thoroughly grounded in that more ultimate support and direction that can be apprehended in but not identified with any particular expression.

Those introspective and searching enough to be reading this chapter are unlikely to be afflicted with this kind of hot bondage of super self-investment in one of the particulars of ministry. In fact, they are already all too aware of the perils of this kind of bondage. They can draw the portrait and make the accusation fully as sharply as I have. Perhaps they have been nodding their heads in full agreement over my characterization and recalling individuals whose ministries they cannot admire precisely for the reasons I have described. This sensitivity to the perils of such bondage feeds whatever inclination they already have to avoid self-investment, precisely because such a self-investment is so risky.

127

## The Bondage of Under-Investment

One can avoid the risks of over-committing to the preaching role or any other partial and potentially flawed form of ministry—just as one can avoid the risk and grief of any human relationship—by withholding from it. You stay cool or cynical and uncommitted. You abstain from preaching, or go through the motions, but are relentlessly self-depreciating, either about your own preaching or about preaching in general. But this is not a freedom. This is another form of bondage, *cool* bondage. You are driven to rehearse the perils and flaws of preaching, to advertise and protect (and to avoid testing) your own ministerial virginity, as it were, your identification with the ideals and the ultimate.

You need to prove your alignment with, your dependence on, the highest standards, to protect your purity by withholding from any investment in actual give and take. The maneuver is like that of the child who comes to feel assured of being connected with parents only by internalizing their standards and enforcing these on self and others, to the point of aloofness from any situation that would risk violation—a frozen independence indeed, cool bondage.

If the captive in hot bondage seems preoccupied with the techniques of sermon construction and delivery, so may this cool captive, but for different reasons. The former is preoccupied because satisfactory performance supports one's feeling of well-being. The latter is more likely to be anxiously forestalling poor performance. This captive identifies with the ultimate values and criteria by imposing them, in advance, on one's own behavior. The impossible ideal of an absolutely perfect sermon looms large, and you cannot venture a word without recognizing how far short you fall. So, too, you are particularly alerted to the disapproval of your hearers, or perhaps their fawning approval for what you know all too well are the wrong reasons. Words come slowly in preparation and subdued in delivery. Investment in each word is almost too risky to warrant spontaneous flow or forceful enthusiasm, for each word may be the wrong word or, at the very least, preclude others. A sentence is hardly begun before a dozen necessary qualifications flood the mind. One illustration or analogy is hardly fashioned before the mind is flooded with all the ways it fails to fit. And all of the attention and effort these misgivings compel only enhance the agony, because they make you work harder on the sermon, take it more seriously, give it more refined attention than it deserves. Difficulties in investing yourself force more investment in the preaching than is comfortable or justified. Choice of topic and text, organization and development, style of delivery— everything becomes a matter of uncertain conviction, because of uncertain commitment. Commitment to the form of preaching, or to any of its forms, remains elusive because to do so risks alienation from that which you would express and foster through preaching.

But here is the final despair and irony: To be loyal to the ultimate purposes of ministry, there can be no adequate self-investment in any expression of ministry. But this inability, on behalf of the ultimate purposes of ministry, is precisely what sabotages loyalty to the transcendent. The absence of a vigorous style—or any style at all—annuls communication from the pulpit. So does the very inability to take a single idea and, leaving aside the many qualifications and the many companion ideas, to develop it vigorously and thoroughly. Uncomfortable preaching with particulars and in partialness, one cannot preach at all the important truths in whose name one abstains from partial and limited statement.

## Freedom

But there is also a kind of freedom of investment. Here is the minister who throws herself into her preaching—or any other activity—with all the vigor and enthusiasm and verve of the "hot" captive. But *she* knows just as well as the "cool" captive how wrong and partial it can be. So she is as free to abandon or correct or try her preaching again as she was to venture it.

Somehow—and though this "somehow" requires considerable development, I can defer it to later pages and refuse to be inhibited by this fact from trying to state my present point as clearly as possible—this minister finds herself and her vocation centered, assured, and justified on some reliable basis. This leaves her freed from the need to find her justification in either exclusive and blind reliance on a particular form of preaching or the elusive and yearning search for an immediate and direct encounter with the saving and directing ultimate truth, a mystical direct encounter that bypasses any actual forms.

She is able to invest herself in preaching—in a particular style and with a particular topic with particular words to particular people in a particular place—with commitment and vigor as though it were a pure instance of undiluted ministry. Yet at the same time she knows, as a kind of secret divine joke, that this is not so, and that she is treating it only "as though" it were.

This freedom may be illustrated by some very concrete and particular incidents that might arise in preaching. Let us consider three kinds of "disasters" that may be yielded by investment in a sermon, to see what response to the disaster distinguishes between the minister in bondage and the minister who has invested in freedom.

*How one deals in freedom with an analogy gone astray.* Suppose she works hard to develop a theological point with an analogy concerning the relations between parents and children. If someone's after-the-sermon narthex reaction is to quarrel with her theory of child-raising, she will not deny and overlook the failure of communication (as would the first captive, who might simply pass over the remark with a kind of jovial "I'm glad you were listening so carefully," or else find ways to misconstrue it as some kind of development of the point she *did* want to make). Nor will the freely invested minister be surprised or disheartened, as would the second captive, that her best efforts have missed the point and have raised a tangential response. She is not so dependent on evidences of effect and effectiveness that she is forced to believe the effects of the sermon are limited to and measurable by just such reactions. But neither is she so dependent on the sermon she preached that she is afraid to follow, closely and with new investment, this new prospect of ministry now offered to her. What may possibly be so important about child-rearing practices in the life of this parishioner that the question erupts and interrupts in this way? This may well be a new occasion for ministry. Or what was there about the original point that drove the parishioner to the evasive action of discussing the analogy? Perhaps the sermon registered more keenly than he can admit, and here is the point for needed future ministry. Or perhaps the analogy is all the parishioner can understand, and there is a lesson for the minister to learn about how well she is getting her main points across. Wherever the parishioner's remarks may lead, the minister is free to follow, not bound by her past investment in the sermon.

A reason why she does not despair over having worked so hard on the analogy only to have its point lost is her awareness that only by developing the analogy as fully as she did could she have provoked this kind of response. Her investment has borne fruit, even though in an unanticipated form. In the half-invested captivity that might have resulted from her anticipation of the analogy's failure, she would have developed the illustration so timidly that it might well have not seemed real enough and vivid enough either to carry her own point or to provoke the tangential concerns of the parishioner.

But as fully as she may invest herself in these new occupations of ministry, she is free to abandon them too. The parishioner's question may not be revealing matters of great moment, or it may be touching on matters too tender for further exposure at this point. Or maybe he is only making conversation. In following this new lead seriously and with commitment, the minister is not so bound to it, so hoping for results, so needing to use her counseling skills and psychological insights, so eager to improve her next sermon, that she cannot cheerfully and freely abandon this lead too.

*How one deals in freedom with disagreement.* Suppose a preacher feels called to try to interpret to his people the concerns of gays and lesbians for equal rights in matters of employment, housing, and shared property. And suppose this evokes an angry response from a parishioner who is convinced that the Bible opposes same-sex relations and that gays are sexual predators intent on exploiting young boys. The first captive would be likely to deny the contradiction and confrontation. He might dismiss the parishioner and his contention as provincial or misguided or otherwise not really in a position to offer valid challenge to the position the sermon sets forth. Or he might accomplish the same purpose by developing the kind of personal and jovial rapport with the parishioner that "transcends" the challenge by not taking him seriously.

The second kind of captive, if he had indeed achieved this much investment in order to have preached a provocative sermon, would be likely to view the reaction with despair ("Here I can't even register my point with the very person, an influential elder, it is most important to reach") and derive from the episode a lesson not to risk such forthright investment again.

The freed minister may celebrate the fact that he has so vigorously thrown himself into a real issue as to provoke this kind of reaction. But he is also ready to abandon the terms of his statement and take up the matter afresh in terms and with the person as it now presents itself. The new need to minister may be related to (even disclosed by), but be different from, the need for ministry the sermon was intended to address. What do gays and lesbians and their advocacy for equal rights mean to *this man* in his particular situation? This is a new and perhaps urgent matter, which may also require a great deal of new investment to pursue. What sort of fears or worries does this man feel? How has he come so to interpret his own Christian way of life as to feel that gays and lesbians are a threat rather than a potential extension of his Christian vision? How can the purposes of the gay and lesbian activities be meaningfully interpreted to this particular man? These may be the kinds of questions that can now be fruitfully employed. Or perhaps others. Or perhaps none. At any rate, the freed minister stands ready to invest his efforts in the particular forms in which they may present themselves on the particular occasion.

*Out on a limb proving God.* Take the case of a minister who preached on Pentecost, fervently wanting to emphasize the divine foundations of the church and the consequent scope of its mission. She dramatized all the seeming supernatural elements in the second chapter of Acts, especially the multiple languages, reminding her listeners of their own trouble—without God—in learning even one additional language. She pointed out that crowds normally are hostile to such "street-corner preaching," dramatizing instances of this in the congregation's own town, and argued that the receptive response to Peter's sermon proved divine intervention. She made the same argument for the assembly of people from distant cities, contending that without divine intervention such diverse aliens in a strange city would have clustered with their own kind and not come together in one place. She even produced a map suggesting that all the cities represented by Peter's hearers formed a kind of a star, which seemed to be still additional evidence of supernatural warrant. She emphasized the careful construction and subtly effective strategy of Peter's sermon, again arguing that only with divine intervention could such a refined sermon be preached by such a simple—even obtuse—man as we otherwise know Peter to be. In short, she combed through the account of Pentecost to read in it every plausible basis of inference of divine intervention—and maybe even some that were not so plausible. She was determined to prove her point. She impulsively and heedlessly invested herself in it. She went way out on a limb.

After the sermon her people called her on it. "Who wound you up today?" "You forgot to say that people came from fifteen locations. That's the five letters in Peter's name multiplied by the three letters in God." "I was willing to believe you when you started out."

She acknowledged the jibes. "I was on a rampage, wasn't I?" "Okay, I'll use that bit about the fifteen locations next week." "So, I should have quit while I was ahead." She *did* register a few do's and don't's to follow in her future preaching. More significant evidence of her freedom, the following week she began her sermon with a caricature of the preceding week, using the divine multiplication problem her parishioner had ironically suggested. Having conceded in this way her single-track, determined effort to invest the church with sanction, she reflected with them on the implications of such an effort. Did her exegetical dredging betray some doubt on her part as to whether the church *is* God's institution? Perhaps; she confessed to occasional doubts and despair. More likely, it represented the earnestness of her own conviction that the church is God's, combined with the frustration that she felt in stating this clearly and convincingly to the congregation. Then with this frustration acknowledged, she ventured to suggest the various possible bases for commitment to the church as God's institution. She discussed with them the kinds of criteria they might look for in their own church for discovering whether it seemed to represent God's purposes.

Compare this "freed" minister's experience with the kinds of bondage described earlier. The "cool" kind of captive would never have gone so far in relentlessly pursuing a single line of thought as the Pentecost sermon—and therefore would never have gotten beyond it into the fresher and richer insights provoked by it. She would have been locked behind misgivings over venturing specific interpretations. The images of professors back in seminary or critics in her congregation would have hovered over her shoulder, inhibiting any such untoward expression with masses of qualifications, interpretations of the interpretations, and a thoroughly balanced and discreet presentation.

The "hot" kind of captive would have so needed the point she was making and/or sense of effectiveness in making it, that she could never have entertained or acknowledged the rejoinders. She would long since have signaled to her people the rigid needfulness of her investment in her sermons, so they would not have ventured to reply so directly and productively. They would have protested more indirectly—in not discussing the sermon at all with her in the narthex, in dropping out from Sunday morning worship, perhaps in a discreet, timid inquiry as to other interpretations of Acts 2. She could not have come close to accepting these comments on her sermon.

The freed investor described in the incident could throw herself thoroughly into an idea and an argument that must have seemed reasonable and appropriate at the time. But she could also transcend and not be bound to this argument, evidenced by the good humor by which she entertains and apparently welcomes responses, evidenced also by her willingness and ability to profit and correct her understanding of what was realistic and appropriate, but evidenced most of all in her ability to work through the encounter and come out the other side with richer insights.

## Sources of Freedom

What can account for the difference between bondage and freedom? What differences in experiences, attitudes, outlooks, self-understandings could there be between the minister enslaved in either kind of bondage and the minister who has the freedom of self-investment? The customary answer pointed to by the combined weight of our theological and psychological heritage is almost a cliché—but we ought not to be intimidated into a fear of restating it by that either: The minister who can feel assured of life and vocation supported, guaranteed, warranted, accepted, thoroughly rooted and allied with—"justified by"—that which is truly the center and ground of life and ministry is the minister who is free to invest herself because she is free to abandon her investment. She has no need for the kind of self-justification that comes from clinging desperately and blindly to particular accomplishments and investments, nor for the self-justification that comes from clinging desperately and blindly to direct, immediate, and unmistakable evidence of belonging to the ultimate. If one had firm religious faith, one would be free to function more effectively as a minister. If one felt assured of the unconditional unquestioning support of important persons (be they parents, parishioners, or others), one would be freed.

Such statements are true. But they are indeed so commonly and easily stated that they carry little meaning. What actual experience might such statements point to? What is this trust, which makes all the difference? And where does it come from? To what experience or self-understanding might a Christian have reference when feeling an unconditional support and assurance that frees to venture risky investments, risky *vocational* investments and—if there is in fact a distinction—risky *self*-investments?

What is the confidence that permits going out on a limb? The imagery of the risky limb restates the traditional Christian understanding of trust and its resulting freedom and distinguishes this from alternative views. What might it mean theologically to "go out on a limb for God"?

*Guaranteed soft landing.* One might mean that he trusts himself on a limb that may break off because he feels sure that a soft landing is guaranteed him, even if it does break. This is a kind of religious faith that can be called compensating, and has also been called illusory by many. It is a faith that looks outside any present moment of involvement, whatever its possible risks, for a compensating satisfaction or affirmation.

133

Heaven-imagery is one version of such a compensating faith. So is the retreat, or prospect of retreat, into a moralistic self-satisfaction or a mutually congratulatory in-group. It is the freedom a small boy has to provoke the bully of the streets, knowing that if his bluff is called, he can run back into his yard, shut the gate, and count on the support of mother or father. Here is the academic freedom of the professor on tenure. He can venture risky causes and risky ideas because they do not risk his job. He is guaranteed his "chair."

The ministers described above as free enough to risk an investment in their preaching might derive this freedom from their confidence that important personal supports are guaranteed apart from and regardless of their preaching. "Important personal supports" might be *external*, perhaps God's goodwill and one's personal religious salvation, perhaps the love of one's spouse, or parent, or parishioners, or perhaps the endorsement of one's ministry by professors back at school, or colleagues in ministry, or the bishop. Such support is offered "unconditionally," or more likely, based on conditions other than preaching performance (a sense of God's goodwill, perhaps, based on virtuous personal and devotional life; a spouse's love, perhaps based on personal characteristics more apparent at home than in the pulpit; the bishop's approval, perhaps based on limited institutional criteria, etc.). "Important personal supports" might be more *internal*. Perhaps self-confidence and vocation derive from the competence felt in some other role than preaching. One might regard oneself primarily as a counselor or social actionist or community leader or discussion leader and see these as separate enough from preaching that risking the latter does not really threaten the self-assurance based on the former. One is free to feel abandon in, or to abandon, preaching because self- and vocational assurance is elsewhere.

This type of compensating faith undoubtedly works. It *does* yield this kind of freedom for segments of life and for vocations sufficiently isolatable so that disaster in the segment does not seem to threaten disaster to the life or to the vocation. This way of understanding the relation of faith and freedom is undoubtedly a common pattern among religious persons. It is one made particularly popular when the analogy of a psychotherapist's acceptance is used to understand the dynamics of faith: The therapist can supply a freeing, virtually unconditional acceptance (as a patient's parents often have not) because the therapist is isolated in the patient's life and is not threatened or, for that matter, even affected by misdeeds or deficiencies of the patient (as parents were not immune).

This way of gaining assurance and freedom—by segmentation and compensation—may be common, effective, religious, and even psychologically understandable. But is it Christian? And is it thoroughly and effectively freeing? As the pattern is applied to God, it assumes a nurturing God who is remote from the actual affairs of men and women, and unaffected by them, and unsuffering with them. It assumes a God who, like the nurturant mother, is waiting for her young refugee from street brawls, protected and protecting behind the garden gate and off the street. It assumes a God who, like a psychotherapist, conducts an hour of sanctuary once a week or once a day, remote and essentially unaffected by the affairs of the rest of the week.

This pattern of thought assumes a view of self and vocation in which fragmentation and isolation is possible. In the example before us, preaching can be entered into freely—and even, perhaps, lightly and irresponsibly—just because it is separate from the crucial sectors of one's life and vocation. This compartmentalization is alien to the Christian's understanding of the integrity of one's own response to the calls of that God. In the last analysis, such a basis for freedom is not that of a risky investment of self, because the self is not invested or risked. Such freedom is possible only on the edges of life.

*Clinging to the guaranteed limb.* Another way to understand the assurance that gives freedom is to see the assurance as guaranteed, as it were, for certain limbs. The risk is in choosing the limb, for some limbs *do* break off. But if you *do* select the "right" limb, and if you *can* find evidence assuring yourself that the limb is guaranteed, then you can experience the confidence and the resulting freedom. Here is the pietistic confidence in vocation and institutional structure, so long as vocation and structure bear identifiable marks of being "true." So long as you can point to the evidence that you have chosen and performed faithfully, the covenant assures that God will provide. Here the childhood analogy is not that you can run to an ever-available supporting mother, nor that you can guarantee nonalienation from parents by internalizing their sanctions. Instead, the analogy is that you can guarantee parental approval and the sense of nonalienation by performing those particular behaviors that they are known to endorse and sanction: get good grades, don't smoke, brush your teeth, fasten your seat belt.

The preacher might be assured by memories of her seminary professors' instructions, by the unexpected ingenious interpretation she finds for the text, by the smoothness with which the idea develops, or by other signs she may interpret as ratifying her enterprise—with a confidence that she is on the right track. Hence she can pursue it freely, heedless of more routine cautions and risks.

This view, too, is common, psychologically understandable, and religious. But again there is a question as to how Christian it is and how truly effective. This, too, assumes a compartmentalization that breeds irresponsibility. It assumes a bargaining God, an almost finite God who rules over some segments of life, but not others. It assumes a God

135

somehow related to the risks and the defeats of most persons in most areas of life. Again there is a real question as to how much self is invested and how much risk.

*Freedom as obligation.* There is another basis for understanding free and risky investment that is not unknown. This is to regard freedom as a kind of duty. We have learned that real faith is supposed to generate freedom. If such freedom is the hallmark of faith, then you ought to demonstrate your faith by gritting your teeth, rolling up your sleeves, and forging ahead in earnest freedom. You go out on the limb because it is the thing to do. Here is the child of the enlightened parents, struggling fiercely to be spontaneous and creative, because this is what they want for you—unlike the "unenlightened" parents who insist on neatness. Here is the compulsively rebellious adolescent, determined to demonstrate freedom.

But such "freedom" as this partakes of a grim lawfulness and calculation that itself contradicts freedom. Acting the role of the one who is freed does not induce the spirit of freedom but only locks you into the role, rigidly. You respond to the preconception of what freedom is like and to the sanctions that enforce it, not to whatever new occasions may present themselves and beckon free, creative pursuit. You go out on the limb because the going out is important, not because the limb is important.

*Assurance is in the breaking.* In none of the above understandings is there revealed clear understanding of a redeemer God who acts in the midst of rupture and alienation—the breaking off of limbs. This is the freedom of one who moves out on a limb, not in spite of the possibility it may break off, but because of it. One moves freely into risks and crisis knowing that in—and perhaps only in—crisis and disaster is there prospect of new revelation and new creation and new relation. We have learned that one is most loyal to the creative potentialities within oneself and within others when venturing beyond the confines and into the risky. Adam and Eve did not really become selves and neither do children until they risk exercise of the freedom that is theirs. Even when the risk turns out badly, as it often does, there is still more real selfhood—which is itself a kind of faithfulness to the Redeemer God who is also the Creator God—than without the risk.

Here too is a cliché, an apocalyptic and existential cliché. What content can it have? One analogy is with the child subject to parental punishment, who also finds that this punishment does not jeopardize the relationship with the parents, but builds new relationship. The punishment itself is something they want to and do share with the child, to talk about, to reflect about, to interpret; in *this* sharing is a renewed and vitalized relationship and support, firmer and more intimate than that broken by the punishment and the misbehavior that produced it. Yet without having ventured in the old relationship to the point of punishment there would not have been the new to share.

Another analogy is the psychotherapy patient who ventures to expose himself to the point where anxiety and dread take over, and he must balk at further self-disclosure, displaying what the therapist will know as resistance. But the resistance becomes the focus of the psychotherapy, the promise of dynamic engagements, the basis for therapeutic progress; if the patient never resisted, the therapy hour would go smoothly, and the therapy would make no progress.

Or it is like the married couple who venture to expose themselves in increasing intimacy of relationship, knowing they are leading themselves to friction and failure—and if they can, there will be keener intimacy and trust than would ever be possible without it.

It is when the religious pilgrim ventures beyond the comfortable and into the risky and real grappling with faith that she is eventually driven to the despair and breaking point: "Lord, I believe, help thou my unbelief." The Christian—the follower of the cross—is freed to risk because she knows that help comes especially at the breaking point.

From this point of view the preacher is free to throw herself unreservedly into preaching not from confidence of being spared catastrophe if the sermon fails but from confidence that maturity of faith and self and ministry—for oneself and for one's congregation—lies in working through the catastrophe. The preacher fully develops insights with all the energy and verve and resources and talents that can be mustered and hopes the congregation can respond in equal freedom. In this encounter may be disaster, and beyond the disaster, growth.

# 11

# Counseling in the Wilderness

*Then Moses ordered Israel to set out from the Red Sea, and they went into the wilderness of Shur. They went three days in the wilderness and found no water.*

Exodus 15:22

*Then Jesus was led up by the Spirit into the wilderness to be tempted by the devil.*

Matthew 4:1

The verses above are surely two of the most abrupt and realistic of the Bible, touching the heart of a minister's experience—the discovery that the minister is mostly in a wilderness, that ministry is in that wilderness.

In the first verse the Hebrew people have just made their decisive move, out of the captivity of Egypt and through the Red Sea, with all its strenuous terror. Now safely on the other side, they sing psalms of praise and thanksgiving, appropriate for having entered into the promised land, and they dance. For twenty-one verses of chapter 15 of Exodus they celebrate. Then they turn and look around, and they are in a wilderness of untracked openness and debris of past forays, and they are thirsty and hungry and lost. They want to go back to Egypt. They spent forty years in that wilderness—as long as a minister's career.

In the second verse Jesus has just been baptized—surely the climax of a spiritual journey, a decisive step—and the heavens have opened and pronounced him a most beloved son. The arduous and anguished journey to baptism is ended, and we are ready to see the path to ministry opened before him. Instead, the Spirit leads him into the wilderness, where he is hungry and lonely and sorely tempted to retreat back to the old ways, the display of spiritual power by the sure rules.

In their wilderness—and it seems it could only be so—the Hebrew people found their identity as a people, made contact with their God and found support and direction for their lives. If their passage had been from captivity to the promised land, if the Red Sea had also been Jordan, as the people so fervently wished, they would never have discovered themselves to be the people of God. So also with Jesus: Could he have known himself, and been known, as Son of God had baptism catapulted easily into ministry?

In most of our spiritual and vocational pilgrimages, especially in professional ministry, we readily suppose that a decisive step is *the* decisive step, that liberation from obvious shackles that beset and besot us will launch us into that life and work of faith for which we so yearn while in captivity. While we are in Egypt, the only thing needful is to escape the Pharaoh and get across the formidable Red Sea. Then, over that hurdle, we relax, celebrate, ready to enjoy and till the promised land; and we are stunned to find ourselves stranded in a wilderness bleaker, less charted, and more littered with debris than the land of captivity we just escaped. So we make the breakthrough and answer the altar call or the call to ministry or the call to the first church or the call to the big church; and with all that painful uncertainty and searching anxiety and impatient waiting resolved, we look about and find ourselves in the midst of church or seminary or parish abounding in still more excruciating uncertainty and still more penetrating anxieties.

Even when we make the strenuous breakthrough and liberate ourselves from the constrictions of institution and narrow notions of "call" and ministry and parish, we discover ourselves in the midst of new constrictions and narrow notions, still finding a painful tracklessness and obstructing debris. The assistant who was going to free us from administrative hassles compounds them. The spontaneous prayer group that was freed, and freeing, of agendas and structures takes a lot of attention to keep it going. Our day off is unaccountably (or all too accountably) beset with urgent distractions. We may break out of the confines of the parish altogether. But if we go into experimental ministries, we find them all the more beset with trackless chaos demanding we sponsor structure, or if we go into institutions like hospitals, we find them burdened with chaotic, ramshackle structure. Wilderness all. We want to go back to Egypt, sometimes back to the sure and simpler, though constricting, ways, sometimes at least back to the sure and simpler vision we had in Egypt of how it was going to be. We try hard sometimes to impose on the wilderness our Egyptian vision of the promised land, but it proves no map for the wilderness, only more constriction and obstacle. There is no way back to Egypt and no way forward to the promised land, except by allowing the wilderness to yield up its own tracks and treasures.

Perhaps the rhythms are seen more easily in smaller moments of ministry. Crossing the Red Sea—what seems, until afterward, the decisive step—may be the fashioning of a sermon, the organizing of a committee, the making of an appointment for counseling. The recalcitrance of text and ideas finally yields to a coherent sermon. The lethargy of members and minister yields to a meeting in which all are agreed to plan Project X. The awkwardness of minister and the resistance of counselee are finally overcome by what seems to the minister a clear mutual commitment to "sit down together and face these things." The Red Sea has been crossed and ministry has been launched! Then the minister looks around and finds that they are in the wilderness: The sermon is misheard and attracts only superficial reaction, and that walk down the aisle afterward seems a longer and narrower passage than through the Red Sea. The committee meeting gets bogged down in delaying wrangling. The counselee comes and shows intense and ingenious resistance to facing serious issues: "I don't quite remember what bothered me so much when we made this appointment."

To me it is as clear as the discoveries in the biblical wildernesses that ministry truly begins when the wilderness is fully entered. The rebuff to sermon, to committee project, or to counseling commitment is a rebuff, and is painful and frustrating to the minister. The minister may well be tempted—it is the most standard response—to recall people to the Egypt of the earlier contract and expectations—to fashion ministry by fashioning suitable partners in ministry—"but you *said* you wanted me to preach and implied you would take me seriously. But you *said* you were committed to this committee project, or this counseling process! Now make good on your contract and stop leaving me stranded!" "Recall and live up to our initial visions and commitments, the plans made back in Egypt."

But the rebuff is also a genuine response, and it calls to be taken seriously and responded to, not denied and ploughed over. The rebuff is a step forward, even if into the wilderness. There is nurture and direction to be found in the wilderness, a message in the mess, manna in mania. If seminaries are arenas of doubt and struggle, not oases of quiet faith, what lessons are to be learned in that struggle that take one beyond the expectations of faithful serenity and settlement? What does the wilderness have to teach that would never be found in the promised land envisioned in Egypt? If the parish, too, is the arena of unwelcome, unexpected, even petty, struggle and contention quite unlike the established people of God one may have thought promised, what lesson, what summons, is to be heard in *that* wilderness? If experimental non-parish ministry, or administrative assistant, or prayer group, or day off founder on unexpected administrative scurrying, what is the lesson therein? *Why*

141

do minister and people seem to attract or need to tolerate such intrusive busy-ness? What need for cover or crutch may be signaled by this busy-ness and may therefore be calling new ministry either to self or to others? A casual response to a sermon may well reflect ambivalence toward the message, and ambivalence signals an emotionally important reaction. So also with the committee wrangling and the counseling resistance. If a topic seems so hard to remember or to talk about, it must touch something deep. The very struggle to speak and keep in focus rather than suppress and blur is an important one, to be heard and joined by the minister. When that is done, then the journey is begun.

No one knows where it will lead. Frequently the old ways and old visions of Egypt will seem more than attractive, for the present wilderness is real. The possibility of discovery does not make the wilderness attractive or easy. It is uncharted and full of debris, stumbling, and hunger. The suffering is real. The minister *does* feel stranded and emptied and alone and lost. That's the way it is!

## Lured into the Wilderness

Joseph Fischer had a special reason to feel annoyed and devastated—"wildernessed"—by Janet Snyder's no. Only the day before she had not only said yes to his ministry, she had said please. Janet had said that she had urgent problems to discuss about her marriage and needed to see Joe immediately. It was an important breakthrough, or breakout—out of Egypt and through the Red Sea—for her to open herself this much to reflection and counseling, for Joe to feel he had elicited this much trust and rapport. He didn't hesitate to take the trip through the Red Sea to the promised land. He arranged a time inconvenient to him in order to accommodate her. Then they both discovered that she had little or nothing to say.

To be lured by promises of being needed and then to be stranded is the most devastating of experiences for a minister. And when done at the hands of a woman, it is the most devastating of experiences for a man. More stark biblical images than the wilderness may suggest themselves: Samson at the mercy of the seductive then disempowering Delilah. When men ministers speak of the church as "she," they may be recognizing or setting the stage for their feelings that the church is seducer and castrator. "Give me your best; I need it and want it," she first seems to say. But that soon becomes, "Give me your best; I only want to take it away from you." Yet God still dares to ask ministers to attend to the needs of the one who is wreaking such devastation; not just to overlook the attack but to in-look it, to look into the wilderness for its own tracks.

Janet Snyder was middle-aged. The last of her children had left home, and she was vigorously experimenting with ways to invest her obvious energies and talents. She was increasingly active in the church and was sampling a new career with a part-time job and talked of returning to school. Two or three times at coffee hours and before and after committee meetings she had made remarks to Joe about strain between herself and her husband. She talked of disagreements, of feeling constricted by some of his expectations that she stay home. "I do have to live my own life, and he is not the center of it, even if he thinks he is." Joe listened well. One day she called Joe and said she must see him as soon as possible. Her tone was annoyed and strong, and she said, "I must be making some decisions soon." Joe felt her grievances against her husband were coming to a head. She seemed urgently to need to unburden herself. He agreed to cut short his supper the next night and to see her before a committee meeting at the church.

Janet started out a bit awkwardly. "I have been wondering all day just what I would say to you; I wonder really why I want to see you." Such a slow windup was appropriate and standard to any difficult conversation, and Joe waited. But the windup persisted, and the pitch never came. Janet *did* talk about her marriage: She made an inventory of her husband's fine qualities and did not happen to include any other qualities. She described with unalloyed appreciation his support for her new career, how he had helped her to find a job, and how he was offering her a new car if she needed it. "He is so sweet and so supportive." She reaffirmed her commitment to the marriage and her intention that any new career not interfere with it. Joe recognized this dilemma of balancing marriage and a career—of being fair to husband and to self—as a real problem, and he tried to help Janet think through these questions, to clarify her priorities, and to be aware of risks and options. But he also recognized that this was not an urgent problem; the feelings she had expressed the day before, of being aggrieved and on the brink, were not present in this conversation. She had called him to help her deal with a crisis that she was not now experiencing, or at least talking about.

Joe could have focused on the no. He could have called Janet's attention to his own setup and letdown and her role in producing it. "Do you often lead men on in this way, then let them down? Does this illustrate something that is a difficulty in your marriage?" This is one way for a minister to make some use of his hurt, his personal wilderness. It is a kind of psychological inquiry, a common one, but certainly not the way I am recommending here. It turns the attack back on Janet. It makes her feel wrong or sick for saying no. It does not invite her to explore her no, only to explore his hurt and to feel guilty for it. In the common way of men relating to women, it is defining the episode in terms of his experience, assuming that disruptions in the situation are due to the woman's defects or disease. It's not much different from the complainings of the

Hebrew people to Moses: Now see what you have done to us. Psychological sophistication encourages this kind of defense by diagnosis; I do not. The no is a signal of distress, a clue to be explored. For the minister to focus literally on the no and take it at face value is to understand it only for what it means to the minister.

Joe could have tried to recall Janet to her yes. He could have reminded her of the agenda she once had for this meeting and asked her to stick to it. He had kept to his contract by arranging the time; she should keep hers. He could have coached and prompted her: "You said you wanted to get together and talk about grievances and about decisions. Let's do it."

Instead, he called attention to the discrepancy as such and made it clear that it was a discrepancy they shared. The yes and the no were both valid and important and so was the discrepancy between them. This discrepancy must have a meaning that was important to both of them. In any case, it was a discrepancy they now shared. He was curious about it and respectful of it and of Janet.

"You seem to be in a different mood today from yesterday," Joe said to Janet. "Yesterday you were agitated and had some intense things pressing on you. Tonight you seem calmer and seem to be searching for something to focus on." Can such a remark be uttered and be heard as descriptive and not as judgmental, as an expression of curiosity, not of scolding, as an expression of something they now share rather than as something that makes them adversaries? Can Janet feel that Joe is scratching his head, not pointing his finger? Most important, can Joe successfully invite them to be open to what is new rather than to be governed by what is old, to be hearing the call to ministry that is in the very disruption of the old contract of ministry? No less than the Hebrew people with Moses and no less than Jesus, Janet and Joe are in a new wilderness together. It is a wilderness promising new affirmations. Somewhere in the very fact that Janet and Joe's conversation is different today from what they expected, and more wandering, there are clues to insight and to healing; but the affirmations are not yet visible and cannot become so until the expectations of the past, even of yesterday, are severed, their sovereignty overthrown. They really are in a wilderness, and only by facing that fully can they discover the life and call and ministry that awaits them in it.

Joe wants to face starkly that they are in a new wilderness, that they have left behind the expectations and covenants of yesterday. "It hardly seems now worth rushing our suppers for." The real risk is that he will sound judgmental, not descriptive, that he will seem to be complaining (emphasizing the no) or coaching (trying to return to the yes), not really accepting where they *are*—in the wilderness. What he wants is to invite them both to leave that old contract and its debris well behind and to explore, together and in trust, the new dilemma in which they find themselves. Can he really mean it, and can she really hear it as a call to explore this new wilderness for its new but as yet undisclosed signs of hope and of direction?

In a sudden moment of unexpected abandonment, unforeseen wilderness, can Joe really mean what he firmly believes as a more general principle? From the pulpit—above it all—Joe can believe and preach that God reveals and calls and guides and supports in the wilderness and the brokenness of life, in the debris of old covenants, in the wandering of wilderness. He can warn how tempting and also how ultimately frustrating it is to want to return from the wilderness back to Egypt, to the safety of former guidelines and habits and covenants. But what if one finds a real wilderness in one's own life? What if one has hurried supper to meet a crisis and finds no crisis, only a woman who says, "I wonder why it was I needed to see you?" Then Joe really knows what it is like to want to revert to the old covenant and to make it govern and redeem the occasion: out of the wilderness and back into Egypt. Turn these stones into bread. "Let's get back to business, Janet."

The Janet who says no to the previous contract is not "less" than the Janet who said yes to it, though that is how it feels to Joe, who wants to bring her back "up" to the contract. The Janet who says no is *more* than the Janet who said yes. She is a new Janet, someone to get newly acquainted with. For there is substance, texture, richness, and much meaning and guidance in the no. In the no is where Janet is most presently and immediately living, in the no is where she is most emphatically and energetically addressing the important matters of her life. One need hardly be surprised that the address is resistant and ambivalent and disruptive; most serious attention to serious matters is.

So Joe did not need to stop and mock at the apparent no to something old. He wanted to get acquainted with the meaning of this new response, and he supposed Janet did too. In the no is where she was most emphatically and energetically addressing the important matters of her life. Joe did not know what these were. They were in the no, obscured by it. But they *were* in the no—in the know?—their presence signaled by the no. So he called their attention to the no, looking squarely at it as the no it was, to identify it and to accept it as a signal.

"You seem to be in a different mood today from yesterday. Yesterday you were agitated and had some intense things pressing on you. Tonight you seem calmer and seem to be searching for something to focus on. Now it hardly seems worth rushing our suppers for." He meant to accept the no as a signal of something important in her and not as a rebuke that she had said no. He really wanted to focus on the no, on today's calmness and rambling after yesterday's urgency, as what was real and important and meaningful. That is what they were sharing and what they could talk about as important clue and path. He did not want to focus on yesterday's yes, on the agitation and the "intense things," as though they were what was important, and as though they were not having meaningful conversation until they could return to yesterday's conversation, yesterday's contract.

If Janet had been made to feel defensive, rebuked for the no or re-called to the contract, then she might have responded by denying the no ("I *am* talking about important problems in my marriage") or explaining the no in trivial ways ("I guess I'm tired at the end of a long day") or denying the contract ("I wasn't so sure what was bothering me yesterday either") or explaining away the contract in trivial terms ("I guess my busy schedule just made me tense yesterday. I should have had a good drink and not bothered you").

But instead of feeling rebuked or recalled, she felt invited to explore this discrepancy as of interest and of import. "Yes, I do feel more sub-dued tonight, less adventurous, less like exploring new things, and more like settling down in a nest and being comfortable." She accepted Joe's reflection of her changed mood and sharpened it with her own words. These sharper words represented a new step inward, toward meaning, from the superficial calmness where they started.

Ready to take still another step, Joe picked up some of these sharper words and kept them focused on their immediate situation, still on the no she had said to their original contract. "Yesterday it seemed you wanted to spend time with me to strategize, explore, maybe even hold a war council, but tonight it feels more like you want me to help you build a nest and huddle in it and count your blessings."

"I do have so many blessings, don't I," Janet conceded, acknowledging that he touched her mood correctly. "A good marriage, a husband who cares about what I'm doing and supplies the money to do it. Just this morning he was asking me closely about how I was going to spend the day."

And then, while Joe was silent, Janet reflected on the discrepancy that he had pointed to and that she had begun to hear in her own remarks. "But you are right; yesterday I was feeling myself more of an independent person, not so much just his wife, and I was feeling some restrictions and some anger in the marriage, not just comfort. Yesterday it felt a little more like a prison and not just a nest."

"And yesterday you would have been annoyed, not reassured, by his close scrutiny of your day's schedule." Joe tried to show that he was thinking her thoughts with her.

"Yes, yesterday I was wanting to be more of an independent woman and even be willing to face some of the things in my marriage that were perhaps holding me back." And then Janet added with a sigh, "But all that seems lost today."

"No I don't think it's lost. I think it's covered up." Joe shared with Janet explicitly his conviction that the no was more, not less, than the yes, that the seeming "loss" of the spirit of yesterday was itself a meaningful event. "I think you still just as much want to be the independent woman and to face difficult issues in your marriage. For some reason, today you *also* seem to want to play the role of the comfortably married woman." The particular contours of the no were becoming clearer to both of them.

"Why would I feel that way especially today?" She accepted the well-focused invitation to look for meaning in the change.

"I don't know." Joe really *didn't* know. He only had the conviction that her change, her no, was a signal to something meaningful in her life. And he had tried to say so clearly and acceptingly.

"Well, there was an awkward thing that happened this morning." Janet let her mind go into her marriage and look for clues. "I was up late last night writing some letters. I have some friends to keep in touch with who are very important to me. And when he got up this morning he noticed that I had left the desk light on. And he was furious. I know how important it is to him to keep lights turned off, and I should have been more careful."

"You sound like a bad girl," Joe said, keeping the focus on her subdued, self-effacing posture of the day, which apparently began with this morning episode.

"Well, he was very angry."

"And that really got to you this time. Sometimes I have heard you talk about his fussing in a different perspective, as a restriction you resented. But this time you have it that he is right and you are wrong." Again, Joe's strategy was to focus on the discrepancy, on what was new and, although disrupting and unwelcome, probably very meaningful.

"He was shouting in a way that I don't think I have heard before." His anger really frightened her. "I didn't know what he might do."

"You were afraid he might hit you?" Joe probed.

"No, no…but he might leave me." Janet suddenly realized this as she blurted it out. And she was suddenly sobbing with the realization. "That's it, he has seemed so patient and accepting, but if all that anger is there, perhaps it's been building, and he just may do something about it."

"And that would leave you abandoned." Joe could understand such anguish especially keenly.

Then the conversation went on, usefully and intensely and intimately about Janet's fears of being left alone, both by her husband and by others earlier in her life, and of the desperate anxiety such rejection and such loneliness raised for her. It became a crucial and valuable counseling session about fears that frequently afflicted and immobilized her. These fears and the possibility of dealing with them in counseling were discovered precisely by attention to the effects of these fears as they showed up in her no to Joe, her repudiation of the earlier contract. Janet was immobilized from meeting her own and Joe's expectations of what their after-supper session would be, just as she was frequently immobilized from doing other things she wanted to do and for precisely the same reasons. In her "nesting" posture with Joe there was a small sample of an important reaction that was frequent in her life. By paying attention to the fact that it was meaningful to her, even without knowing that meaning and by ignoring the disruptive meaning it had for him, Joe was able to help her see and deal with something important in herself.

Janet *was* bringing her full self to Joe for counseling. The full self happened to be even fuller than their first contract had anticipated. By paying attention to that new fullness, as disruptive and disconcerting as it was, Joe was able to be a counselor to Janet as she was. They both had had expectations when they made their appointment—expectations formed in Egypt—of how they could be counselor and counselee for each other. If they had stuck with those expectations and tried to fulfill them, they would have become battlers, a scolder and a defender. By giving up their expectations of how they would be counselor and counselee and by dealing directly with the new wilderness in which they found themselves, they were able to be counselee and counselor in more profound and meaningful ways.

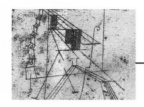

# 12

# Shepherding Programs or Getting Lost Together?

*And the Pharisees and the scribes were grumbling and saying, "This fellow welcomes sinners and eats with them." So he told them this parable: "Which one of you, having a hundred sheep and losing one of them, does not leave the ninety-nine in the wilderness and go after the one that is lost until he finds it? When he has found it, he lays it on his shoulders and rejoices. And when he comes home, he calls together his friends and neighbors, saying to them, 'Rejoice with me, for I have found my sheep that was lost.'"*

Luke 15:2–6

"Be the good shepherd!" is what ministers most often hear and tell others to hear in the parable of the lost sheep. "Be gentle and strong. Above all, able! *Find* the lost sheep and bring them home, in triumph and to plaudits." "Yes, yes," I answer. "I want to be like the compassionate and virile good shepherd, like Jesus. We all do. Others are weak and loveless, and I must be strong and loving and help them." So the good news of the gospel becomes a burden, the vision of God's kingdom becomes a blueprint for my labors, a criterion for my accomplishments. What is offered to me as a free gift becomes a task I must perform. My anxieties to guarantee my own place in the kingdom compel me to take that place as host (which always compels me to make others be guests) rather than to believe that I am welcome as guest.

But the parable contains another message, probably the one Jesus intended: "You have a good shepherd." When you are lost, you will be found; alone, you will be joined; cast down, you will be lifted up; loveless, loved. Even you (even if you are a minister, even if you are an established member of an established church) may be weak and wandering, aimless and inept, without forfeiting your place in the kingdom. Indeed, when you are lost, let it be just so. There, too—no, there especially—is God's love and ministry.

## Yes-Saying: First Commitments

Tom Goddard vividly remembers when he first got the idea for the day-care center. It was one of those rare "ah-ha!" experiences, when suddenly everything seemed to come together in his mind, and he knew he had a good idea. Tom was glancing through his denomination's monthly publication when his eye caught the short report of a day-care center organized in the parish house of a downtown church. Although Grace was a suburban church, in a very different community, Tom could immediately see exactly how and why Grace should undertake this. He saw the project unfolding spontaneously before him, meeting many needs in the church and in the community, and giving his own ministry a needed shot in arm. He knew that the people and the church would enthusiastically adopt it as a good idea, and he was right; they did. It met the needs that he and they had to be good shepherds.

There are many reasons that made Tom—and very soon, many of his church members—give such a quick yes to this project. It is important to look at some of these reasons here in order to recognize the degree of commitment the project first evoked from the congregation and also to recognize the depth of anguish and frustration when the people began to say no. A project with this many reasons for it and so much initial enthusiasm for it simply ought not to develop the no-saying it did.

Tom had a long-standing commitment to a ministry of service to the community—to be a good shepherd—and so did Grace Church; there had been much talk about this when the pulpit committee first sought him out, and there had been much rhetoric in his installation service about a minister and people together finding avenues of faithful service in their community. But these commitments had found little expression while Tom had been at Grace Church, and the church's ministry was largely self-contained and self-directed. Most projects of outreach into the community seemed too grand and too fearful.

But the day-care center seemed just right. It was a modest and feasible way to be good shepherds. The day-care center project readily bypassed many of the suspicions and fears on which previous ventures in mission had foundered. Children are intuitively appealing, their need for care is personal and individual, and they would be coming into the parish house to be served. The project asked people to give services and time, with which they were more generous than money. Though it was going to reach people outside the church—there were few working mothers in the church—they were people living in their same suburb who seemed not greatly different in lifestyle and values; after all, the mothers were working. It was going to use resources of the church and activities already familiar; the day-care center would be much like the Sunday school. In short, the project was a meaningful venture at community service, but one modest enough to minimize apprehension and to maximize enthusiasm in the congregation.

So Tom Goddard was enthusiastic about this project, and justifiably so. This was something the church should and could and would do. Tom could immediately and easily picture the scene in the parish house—the children happy and well cared for and well loved by the many willing volunteers in the space recently redesigned and redecorated by other volunteers from the church. He could picture himself and the congregation emboldened and reassured by this one venture, rediscovering that they *could* exercise an outreach ministry to the community, moving on to other, bolder projects. He could picture the church becoming known, both by its members and by outsiders, as the church with an effective social conscience; this is how he had long envisioned his ministry. He could picture the attention the day-care center would get in the local newspapers, in the denominational monthly, and maybe in his seminary publication. "When he has found it, he lays it on his shoulders and rejoices. And when he comes home, he calls together his friends and neighbors..."

In his enthusiasm, in these hopes and daydreams, and in the care and energy with which he went about introducing the program to the church, Tom obviously had an investment in it. By no means all of his personal or vocational eggs were in this one basket; but he was trusting some substantial part of himself to the project. He would feel more faithful in ministry, more fulfilled in vocation, a bit more easy in conscience—more ready to hold his head up as the minister he wanted to be before his congregation, his colleagues, his seminary professors, and his God—if this project succeeded.

Tom Goddard not only invested his enthusiasm and his daydreams and his hopes and his intentions for effective ministry. He also invested his skill. He was a skillful and careful minister, a *good* shepherd. He had identified a project that he knew would be attractive and acceptable to most people in his congregation. He carefully identified the individuals and the groups with whom it would be important to share his thinking. He patiently spent time with these people, introducing his ideas to them, hearing them out. He anticipated the questions each would have and had thought out his own responses. He was open and ready to let them modify and refine his ideas. He thought ahead to know exactly what further assignments and responsibilities he wanted to ask each person to undertake. He anticipated just how much and just how little direction each person would want and need, and he had some practical advice—whom to see, what to say—for those who were going to need and heed it. Soon Tom Goddard and his people were in genuine and vigorous partnership on this project. If asked, the people would have remembered it was Tom's idea in the first place, but they would have insisted that it was now their project, part of the ministry of Grace Church, not just part of Tom's ministry. Tom was a skillful and careful minister.

Tom's skill, like the modesty and attractiveness of the proposal itself, is important to emphasize here, not just so we can understand and believe the ready and enthusiastic yes with which the congregation first responded. Remembering Tom's gentle skill will also help us better savor the misery and mystery of the no when it begins to appear. When I begin to describe the no—the resistance and the apathy and the objections and the sabotage—that began to cluster around this project and to smother it, you may react at first with a feeling of easy recognition: "That is the kind of opposition social activists always get in churches." But Tom Goddard was not a stereotypical social activist. He did not deserve the rebuff that is deserved by the naïve, roughshod social activist who, with the façade of prophet, angrily and arbitrarily inflicts on people judgments and demands that they are unprepared to comprehend. Tom received the rebuff without deserving it; thus the depth of the anguish and frustration and cause for anger and resentment Tom experienced.

However, that he received the rebuff without deserving it is precisely what opened the way for ministry and guided it. That the rebuff could not be attributed plausibly to anything he had done freed him from defensiveness and guilt. More important, that the rebuff could not be attributed plausibly to anything he had done is precisely what prompted his query about where the rebuff *did* come from. It came from within the people and carried messages about them, messages about matters in their inner lives that invited and required ministry, messages about their inner lives that guided that ministry. The inappropriateness, the unfairness of the no, then, is exactly what induces misery and exactly what induces ministry.

But before the people began to say no—and thereby to frustrate the minister and to invite and guide ministry—they said yes, a resounding yes. They, too, wanted to be good shepherds and welcomed this way to be so. The official board approved the project, not routinely, but with enthusiasm and with their own ideas. The fourth- and fifth-grade Sunday school classes readily agreed "to share our rooms with other kids," cleared off their bulletin board, put up a welcome sign, and made plans to come visit "the other kids." A modest, low-key campaign yielded pledges of enough money to support the project. Members of the house committee spent two weekends building some supply closets and repainting one of the rooms and made plans for designing and building some climbing bars outside when the weather got better. A "grandmother's club" readily organized and became the core staff of volunteers for care and for transportation. A director was hired, and one trustee readily took care of the necessary approval by the health authorities and the fire marshal. The teams that called in homes to invite children came back speaking happily about the chance "to meet new people." Members of the congregation were proud of the attention in the local newspaper, and people frequently were heard bragging proudly to their friends about the project.

The yes was resounding. Minister and people seemed to be in full and enthusiastic partnership. The minister had taken the first step, but the people soon were in stride with him. So it went for several weeks.

## No-Saying: Resistance Emerges

Then the signs of resistance appeared, so familiar to any minister as perhaps not to be noticed at first. Resistance seems the normal way of life in the church, and perhaps it is. The first no message that Tom recalls came quite indirectly: The fourth-grade Sunday school teacher said that one of the girls in her class said that her mother said that she shouldn't have to take down her picture from the bulletin board. An irrational and trivial nuisance in the life of the church and in the way of this project, indeed, but the teacher happened to pay enough attention to it to mention it to Tom. Tom had managed to convey to the teacher the impression that such things were important and could be constructively responded to. And Tom happened to pay enough attention to the teacher's report to call on the mother to see what was up.

153

This was a family on the edges of the church and one that had not been involved in the day-care center planning in any way. What Tom learned from that mother gave him clues that helped him understand, as he might never have done otherwise, many of the other signals of resistance that were shortly to appear. The mother unleashed a barrage of indignation: Her daughter ought not to have to give up things for "those others"; her daughter ought not to have to go visit "those others." As Tom listened, for over an hour, he realized that he had never before quite sensed the precariousness with which some people clung to their own station in life, a precariousness easily threatened by the presence, especially by the moving presence, of those a notch or two below on the social ladder. Her life was precariously bastioned; mixing and yielding to lives that were noticeably different was very threatening. She felt a lost sheep with a vengeance and so tried hard in her own way to herd. (If Tom recognized himself in this posture, it wasn't conscious—yet.) Her needs for focus and for affirmation, for the assurance and direction of the gospel, were too overwhelming to be addressed decisively in one call. But by neglecting to defend the plans for the bulletin board and for visiting, and by hearing and opening and accepting her needs, Tom did a lot.

Being moved in on and supplanted by "others" was not the only threat Tom was to hear about in the coming months. But having heard the mother out at length, he was far more attuned to the frights and the needs within this and forthcoming signs of resistance. Another no was indeed forthcoming, most of it subtle, much of it seeming to be standard, pure no, pure resistance, without any obvious message. Tom listened anyway. Planning meetings were less well attended, but "this is a busy time." Some pledges were unpaid, and the workers did not come back to finish their painting or to build the jungle gym. But such looseness to commitments may seem such a standard way of life in a church as not to attract notice or invite inquiry. Tom wondered what the people might be communicating by this de-commitment, but there was no easy opportunity to inquire or to respond. Perhaps thanks to the fourth-grader's mother, Tom was more ready to suppose that there *was* something important behind this resistance and within it and less ready simply to respond with his own grief for being stranded. To a friend he found himself musing not just about what the apathy meant to him, a letdown after a setup, but also about what it meant to the people. When he said to his friend *"Why* do they back down?" he meant the Why? at least as much as genuine inquiry as he meant it as protest; his Why? was an honest Why? and not just an angry one.

But some of the forms of resistance were more revealing. Some of the members of the "grandmother's club" were willing to be open with each other, with Tom, and with some of the working mothers. "Sometimes their hair isn't even combed in the morning," they would say to each other. To Tom it would be, "I just don't get as much fun out of this as I thought I would. It's hard to get acquainted with some of the kids. I guess I'm getting old. I used to get along well with children." And to the mothers they were more controlled but clear: "You are thirty minutes late picking up Elizabeth. But that's perfectly all right. I'm sure you had a good reason." The differences in lifestyles were more disconcerting than anyone had supposed. Some of the grandmothers began to drop out of their work.

Tom felt a personal disappointment. He had especially delighted in the warm enthusiasm these older women had offered the project. He had spent considerable effort and tact in recruiting them, and their response was rewarding to him and reassuring that the project was a good one and would work well. The initial warmth of their concern for the children had made him feel that this would be a day-care center with a difference because it was a Christian church—good shepherds for Jesus. He envisioned emphasizing this point when he wrote the report he planned for the denominational monthly magazine. So Tom did feel a special disappointment when the women's enthusiasm cooled.

## "Not You!": The Standard Response

At first, he tried to counter this disappointment and this cooling by urging them and by recalling them to their earlier commitment and warmth. "Be good shepherds." His first reaction was to minimize their de-commitment and to minimize the discomfort and distance with which they expressed it: "Oh, you are not so old. You've seen uncombed hair before. These mothers are busy; that's why we are here to help. I think you really enjoyed playing that extra half hour with Elizabeth." Taking their attention away from their discomfort, he tried to return it to their commitment: "Remember how important this is and how we promised each other to stick with it." He cajoled and argued and pleaded as skill-fully and energetically as he had first time around: Don't say no; say yes, again.

His response was the standard response of clergy—so long as they are acting like parents and other good shepherds—of pointing the fin-ger and saying, "Not you! That's not like you. You can't be that way. I will not have you that way. I will call you back to the real you." There was also an element of "Not you, too!" Another traitor or defector whom I did not expect. *Et tu Brute?* You are friend turned antagonist. So I must treat you as the wayward adversary so that I can bring you back to the true ways, my ways.

Tom first practiced the ministry of "Not you" standing strongly as the good shepherd of the day-care center: He was the staunch custodian of that project and of the consciences and commitments that should be directed to it. The strayed would be returned. That was his job; he was the minister.

But Tom was not exclusively program oriented. He was also a pas-tor to these people. He could sense personal distress lurking in their waywardness. So he shifted from the good shepherd of the program to the good shepherd of the women. He began to talk with them privately about the personal problems he thought might be hinted at in their dif-ficulties with the working mothers and the day-care center. He asked one woman if her husband was back to drinking too much again. He was sympathetic toward another about her arthritis. He hinted strongly to another his suspicion that she might be worried and guilty about her pending decision to transfer her mother to a nursing home. To still an-other, he talked about her recent absences from church. Though personal and pastoral, not program oriented, these were all still responses of "Not you." They were still responses of the good shepherd designating the others as lost so that he could herd them and heal them. He was just changing the grounds on which he intended to move them from no-saying to yes-saying.

This shift from program diagnosis and remedy to pastoral diagno-sis and remedy is not taking the no seriously as having its own legitimate meaning and guidance, even call to ministry. It is, instead, to hear the

155

resistance as an indirect cry for help. Perhaps that is what it sometimes is, and it may be good pastoral strategy to be alert to such pleas. But it also may be an arrogant assumption—that a woman's discomfort in a parish program or resistance to it somehow represents "trouble" or "problems" in her life that the minister needs to move in on and to solve. Tom could not respect and attend to the no-saying and listen to the calls to ministry in it because he was still so determined to be a strong minister. He was saying, "You are not yourself when you complain about uncombed hair and all the rest. I will help you be yourself by helping you solve your problems."

The women *were* being themselves in their complaints and their resistance, more fully themselves than in any simple yes-saying of punctuality and steady smiles. And they were being themselves, responding to real events, in the day-care center. To hear the meaning and the call to ministry in their complaints, Tom had to take these complaints seriously, and to take them seriously in the terms in which they expressed themselves: uncombed hair and tardy pickups and all the rest. Tom could not suppose that the meaning was only in undoing the no and making it yes, or that the meaning was off somewhere in personal and family life.

Tom's first response was to suppress the no—and to urge the women to do likewise—to recall and cling to the yes—and to urge the women to do likewise—saying "Not you" to the no. And his second response was to divert the no into a problem to be solved, again saying "Not you" to the no. But he did come to a new response, which was to accept their gentle no as valid, meaningful, important, and to explore it for clues to ministry—and to enable the women to do likewise.

This new response came in a turning point sudden and dramatic enough to be called truly a conversion. Like all conversions, there was a startling moment of confession, a radical letting go of some old, firmly entrenched ways of understanding and conducting oneself—a confession of their wrongness—and a sudden opening up to new ways—a confession of faith and trust in their rightness. If his standard ministerial response was the message of "Not you," the would-be good shepherd, he was able to discover a new and powerful ministry, the ministry of "Me, too," the ministry of becoming a fellow lost sheep. But before this could happen, there happened the dramatic moment of confession and conversion that Tom experienced as "Not me!" He really did feel lost, and said so. It was not just a new posture.

## "Not Me!": Confession and Conversion

It all started with some toy animals left strewn on the floor. Tom overheard a couple of his "grandmothers" gently grumbling about the scatter left behind at the end of the day by the children and their mothers. Tom lost his cool. He strode into the midst of the grandmothers and, wordlessly and vigorously—one might have said even violently—began scooping up toys. When he had an armload, he unloaded them in the toy box, then turned and unloaded on the grandmothers: "It's not all that hard to pick up a few toys. We have to be willing to go a second mile. That's what this project is all about. The kids are not used to having toys like this to deal with, and the mothers are still shy around here. They are still our guests and feel it, and we have to be willing to be the gracious hosts. If we don't have a little grace to share, what's it all for? But you do. I know you do." He peppered the tirade with especially pointed "Not you!" remarks: "If we can't count on you…" "We talked about troubles like this when we started and you said you could handle them…"

The women were stunned, and so was Tom. The outburst spent, they all stooped and picked up the toys, wordlessly and sullenly. Tom found himself on his knees, and some surprising reflections came to him in his stunned state. "What am I doing? That doesn't sound like me. That's not me." He startled himself and the women even more by sharing this "Not me" confession with them. When the toys were all picked up, he stayed on his knees. He didn't apologize, exactly. He just opened himself. As a true and necessary condition for all confessions and conversions, he felt himself safely surrounded by love. His voice was low. "That didn't sound like Tom Goddard. That sounded like a raving maniac. Maybe I am a raving maniac. But I feel more like that scared looking little bunny rabbit you just put in the box."

So, having confessed the "Not me," he began to explore it and to discover the "Me, too." **157**

"I guess your irritations and frustrations, which you were able to express, touched some of my own, which have been dammed up until the dam just burst. I guess I have a whale of a lot invested in this project going well, and I am not so sure—even less sure than you are—that it is going well. If I put you down that hard, I must really have been needing to put myself up, pull myself up. I must have felt way down. I guess I was trying to scold myself, too, to make myself feel better about all the picking up I seem to have to do, going the second mile, filling in the gaps, and smiling about it all the time…Wow, I can't believe I just said that. But it feels right and good. I guess I really have bottled up a lot, and you got it all." Then, for the first time, he looked up with a warm, almost twinkling look, and found some warm looks coming back. One woman came over and put a hand on his shoulder, and others seemed to be doing the same with their eyes. No one spoke for a while. No one seemed to feel the need to talk about Tom and his outburst. What he had said spoke for itself.

When one woman did speak, it seemed irrelevant. It was irrelevant to the content of what Tom had been saying, but not to its mood.

Openness breeds openness, confession breeds confession, grace breeds grace. "Me, too" ministry does not mean that people imitate each other, only that they each share. Deep responding to deep, plight to plight, one woman began speaking, slowly and softly, as in meditation. "How can they be so happy all of the time? My sister was always like that, and I always wanted to be. But I would only get sober and tell her to sober up too. My husband, too; I keep telling him, 'Oh Charles.' I guess that's what I do with the kids, too, telling them to sober up, when I really mean to be telling myself to cheer up…"

158

Her remarks were surrounded by silence too. No one felt the need to "shepherd," to answer plights, to reassure despair. The despair was acceptable and even seemed to breed its own strength. If these were lost sheep huddling together—and they were—the discovery was that even lost sheep have resources to untangle themselves and find their way. The ministry of "Not me" and "Me, too" had an unlocking and refreshing power. Tom and the women felt the power of the Spirit more than in moments of Tom's efforts to conscript the Spirit.

So Tom found himself and found new reaches and depths of ministry in a spontaneous moment of lostness. In this moment of conversion, Tom lost the need to prove himself as good shepherd, to stand over and ahead of others. Seldom again did he respond to de-commitment, subtle or overt, with his previous standard response: calling and recalling people to the commitments he defined for them. Instead, he found the grace to move, even haltingly and unsurely, with the others, to feel a mutuality of need and of search and of grace. By being more open to his own distress and de-commitment—the no mixed with the yes in himself—he could be more open to others' distress and de-commitment and learn to hear the yes mixed with their no. By discovering that he could live with and through his own distress, he could minister with and through theirs. He could find a partnership, a covenant of ministry in shared search, even shared lostness. Tom Goddard discovered new patterns of ministry in himself when he discovered that he could face his own grief and irritation and his need to muffle that grief by insisting on saying and hearing yes, because he could thereby discover new powers in the people, in their grief and irritation.

Now let us look at some of the fruits of that moment of conversion, the effects of a style of ministry of joining lost sheep in their lostness to the point of discovering the meaning in their lostness and evoking the power in it.

## The Ministry of "Me, Too": Lost and Finding

"It's hard to get acquainted with some of the kids. I guess I am getting old…" When one of the grandmothers said this gentle no to Tom, he first heard it as a small piece of the machinery of his project slowing down and needing some oiling and energizing. So he was first tempted to smooth over and to pep up; that was his familiar way of dealing with roughness and downness. So he almost said, "You are just the kind of person these kids need and respond to. I have seen how well you get along with them. They really like you, though some may be shy about showing that."

The most standard way of trying to make people feel *up* is to put down their feelings of being down. People may comply for the moment, but the long-range effect is the "double down."

What the "new" Tom Goddard did say sounded similar, but it had a very different intent and effect. He *did* ask why? But he meant it as a question and not as don't. In effect, "Are you a lost sheep?" He *did* call attention to the discrepancy between the woman's down feeling and his own observation that she, in fact, seemed to be getting along well with the children. But noting the discrepancy was a way of accepting and emphasizing the down feelings, not quashing them. It sounded like "Not you," and it almost was, except this time it really meant "Not all of you," as an invitation to hear more. Noting the discrepancy was a way of looking at the no squarely. The feelings of no and of down are valid and are all the more important and worth exploring because they don't match all the facts. Look for the message written in the roughness, don't try to smooth it over and erase the message. That's what Tom wanted to say when he said, "You do seem down today about the kids, even though it seems that you have been getting along with them pretty well."

"About the kids" was part of Tom's response because he resisted the temptation to be "pastoral," to divert the conversation to a "problem" that was exclusively hers, and not something they shared here and now. Tom was clear that the woman was feeling down *about the kids*.

The woman responded to the gentle inquiry. "Some days I guess they just seem rambunctious." Tom just listened. Whatever the rambunctiousness meant to her would come out. "They get unruly and don't want to quiet down when we ask them, and they don't want to play the games we have planned for them."

"It makes you wonder what you are doing here," Tom reflected. "I sometimes wonder too."

"Well, yes." She accepted the invitation to talk about herself, in this situation. There was some spark of anger, and perhaps she was a little anxious, that the children were different from her and from what she expected. These were the feelings that Tom had heard from the fourth-grader's mother. But beyond these feelings of anger and anxiety about them were stronger anxieties about herself. She wanted to tell Tom about the misgivings that she had that she was different from them and from what they expected. "Children used to be quiet for me, but then I used to be sure what they were like and what they wanted me to do. These seem to get along fine without me. I want to call them to attention and back to our plans, but I am not sure that I should."

These misgivings blossomed into a wide range of distressing concerns as Tom talked longer with her and with others. All of the feelings are common to the aging, but they came out especially strong as these women confronted the day-care kids. For one thing, there was a hint of the anger that Tom heard so strongly from the fourth-grader's mother that "they are taking over." In this case it was more the dilemma of the aging being crowded by new generations rather than one ethnic or economic group being crowded by another. But Tom noted that a profound fear was shared by these workers in the program, by himself, and by an opponent of it; all felt the risk of becoming abandoned sheep. Along with the anger, there were hints of the grief the women felt in losing authority and recognition and affection. They felt abandoned and stranded by the kids, just as Tom felt abandoned and stranded by the grandmothers. Here he and the grandmothers shared a grief, felt fellow lost sheep. More poignant than the anger or grief, there was a touch of envy and perhaps regret. In the rambunctiousness the women felt some "soul," which they had missed in their own lives, even in their childhood. Was there a possibility that these kids, and their mothers, who were taking over the space and time of the grandmothers were making better use of it than the grandmothers knew how to? In the disrupting no that she was hearing the woman was hearing the possibility of a new "call," which also was discomforting. In her ambivalence over whether to give the children tighter or looser rein, she was expressing uncertainty and frustration over the authority they would accord her; she was also expressing uncertainty and frustration over her contentment with her own life.

"We give them all this extra time by taking care of their children, and what do they do with it?" one grandmother once grumbled. "Sometimes I think these women have the right idea," another replied, admiring the greater independence and carefreeness of the working mothers. But for her to say that was to risk saying to herself that she might have lived out some of the wrong ideas. Perhaps the message she heard in the day-care center was not that life was partly passing her by now in her later years, but that life had partly passed her by *all* her years. For a woman to risk saying that, even to herself, she needs a church and a minister. In finding the bonds with others, the shared plights and open understanding that they found in these explorations of their no, these women found a church and a minister.

Tom also heard a remarkable amount of self-righteousness: We always used to take care of our children properly; we get ourselves here on time in the morning; I have worked just as hard as these women have, without getting a salary, before there were machines to do all the housework. The unusual degree of pique and self-righteousness astounded Tom, as it grieved him. He was momentarily tempted to be the "good" shepherd, standing firm and calling the lost back to their proper roles of servanthood. But then he found it natural to abandon his "goodness" and firmness and to look for them where they were. The unusualness, the "wrongness" of the self-righteousness, which grieved him, also signaled to him that something important was lodged in this troubling outburst. He decided to look directly into it, to see if its message could be discerned: "This sounds more like the Girl Scouts' awards day for good deeds than like my grandmothers' club."

"Well, somebody has to appreciate us," one woman retorted, continuing to illustrate the self-righteousness more than exploring it. So Tom kept focusing on this melancholy surprise as a surprise and as a puzzle. "But you know how much you *are* appreciated. I hear mothers say thank you every day. That can't be what all this patting on the back is about."

"Well, sure they say thank you, but you can't be sure they mean it...(Tom waited.) It's often hard to know *what* they are thinking. It's hard to know where they're at."

"Or whether they are there at all." Tom ventured to expand their point and relate it to the complaints he heard about feeling abandoned.

One woman let these feelings carry her along. "Sometimes I wonder where other members of our committee are. Last Monday I hurried dishes and walked down to the church for a meeting, and no one was there when I got there."

161

So the conversation went on. The children and their mothers and others in the project had aroused a mixture of feelings in the women, feelings that were already present in them as women and as members of an older generation, feelings that interfered with their work in the day-care center, feelings that they began to signal in the various ways they were saying no to that work. They were feeling abandoned and stranded, by-passed and estranged, separated from their customary roles and stations, separated from those with whom they wanted to be in helping partnerships, separated from the centers of their own lives, separated from the centers that seemed to control the life about them, separated from possibilities in their own lives, possibilities that the working mothers and their children rekindled tantalizingly. The anguish was especially great because they felt that they had been promised, and indeed deserved, place and partnership. The anguish was especially great because they felt they had lost access to remedy; they were not able to speak to or to be heard by the working mothers (and others), who were the estrangers and estranged. They felt loss and grief, but there was no one against whom they could effectively or properly feel aggrieved.

In hearing all this, the most important response Tom made was to say regularly to himself, "Me, too." As he heard and reflected the grandmothers' feelings, Tom found himself drawn powerfully out of the aloof observer-shepherd role and into these feelings, like suddenly recognizing his own face in the photograph of a crowd scene. "Me, too": He felt his own feelings of abandonment swallowed into the grandmothers' feelings of abandonment; and he no longer felt so alone. "Me, too": He felt his own frustrations and anger and yearning about promises hinted at and broken, opportunities missed (especially those about the day-care center) joined and completed by the grandmothers' wistful yearnings; and it was not nearly so hard to admit how lost he had actually felt. It was possible suddenly to feel an essential part of a genuine ongoing human enterprise—the searching of the lost, the wistful "might-have-beens" of the established—rather than feeling on the margins of things. He felt himself part of those who felt apart, that is, part of the majority. "Me, too": I am being crowded out of the space and role and crowded out of "my" day-care center—just as the grandmothers feel crowded out of "their" day-care center! Together, we feel squeezed out of those spots in which we feel comfortable and competent by others' inability to accept our comfort or to recognize our competence. And in the "Me, too" discovery Tom suddenly felt he again had a place, with the grandmothers. "Me, too": Those who seemed to be strong and against me are not. They are like me, feeling weak and in these feelings *with* me.

This transformation of mood released new energies for new ministry, a ministry of "Me, too": Energies he had spent in trying to reach the grandmothers, or to fend them off, or to establish himself—all of these energies could be released now that he saw that he and they were together, were established, in their lostness. The energies could be spent much more fruitfully and productively for the common good. It was all right to feel the way he did, because others did, too; it was not something to fret over and try to undo. This constant rediscovery of "Me, too" was a profound rediscovery over again of the freeing gospel, a reminder of the "conversion."

Whenever Tom would say "Me, too" to himself and experience the freedom of feeling plights recognized and shared, he would pass along this experience to the grandmothers. Now and then he would drop into the conversation a genuine "Me, too." Every time, the grandmothers would do an emotional double take. They still were not accustomed to seeing their minister on his knees, literally or figuratively. But they *did* readily recognize that, yes, Tom *did* know and feel what they were talking about. The one who seemed at the center of things *did* understand exactly how it was to feel at the margins and forsaken. The one who could have been stalwartly aloof *was* humbled even as they were. The one who could condemn their feelings shared them. They were not isolated but joined, not reproved but matched. In Tom's ministry of "Me, too" they could relax their bristling defensiveness, admit their weakness and yearning, and open themselves to being found and to taking new steps in new directions.

They could afford to take a second look at the working mothers, to perceive their plight and not just their failures as partners. They could relax and accept the diversity of lifestyles; they could reaccept their own, even as they could recognize that there was now also room for others'. At the same time, they were willing to look more deeply at their envy and resentment of the freedoms the younger women had. They could speak more openly and sharingly about these disquieting feelings, for each disclosure was met with another "Me, too." They could identify some patterns they genuinely envied and sometimes even began to imitate—more colorful and freer clothing, less compulsiveness about punctuality, more colloquial language with the children. They could sort out these patterns they envied and sometimes imitated from those against which they genuinely preferred their own styles, their family living patterns, for example. The grandmothers could take a more thorough look at their misgivings about their relations with the children, deepen the misgivings in some respects—the kids simply were unresponsive to their orderly directions—but also deepen the assurances in other respects— the kids did wink affectionately and even make moves to include the grandmothers in their play. The working mothers, who had seemed so intimidatingly strong, so self-contained, even self-centered, could suddenly be perceived as the fearful, marginal, guarded, intimidated people they felt themselves to be.

163

For Tom also ventured to add to his ministry of "Me, too" the ministry of "Them, too." It was far less dramatic for Tom to speak for the working mothers than for himself. But it still made the grandmothers do another double take, to open their horizons and share their lostness, as Tom led them to discover how similar their experience was to that of the working mothers. Tom, grandmothers, and working mothers all felt marginal and alienated, frustrated by broken promises, fearful of slipping competence and eroding identity.

## Routines Redeemed as Ministry

Tom's discovery of the power of the gracious words "Me, too" and his discovery that ministry was in abandoning shepherding more than in shepherding the abandoned changed everything even as they changed nothing. He still did Bible study; he still organized groups of people; he still preached. But he did all of these things in new ways, in a new spirit of sharing—in the communal bond of fellow lost sheep. When living out this spirit yielded, before his very eyes, a new spirit in the life of the people, a compassion and an outreach, a binding and an opening, then he experienced the power of the gospel, quite literally and immediately, in a way he had never known before. The way of the fellow lost sheep was a more powerful way than the way of the good shepherd. The routines that had seemed tedious were redeemed, in Tom's mind and experience, as ministry.

In Tom's newly discovered spirit of "Me, too" ministry, *lost* no longer was a mild invective (like sick or lazy or unfair or sinful) with which to fend off threatening people but rather a term of recognition and acceptance and hope. Once they began to find themselves lost together, they began to find themselves. Exposed and shared, their misgivings about themselves and others began to pare down and began to seek out answers. More and more, they began to seek out others, including the working mothers, more in the spirit of lost sheep wanting to huddle than in the spirit of coercing or enticing—shepherding—others into the fold.

It had always been part of Tom's daydream about the day-care center that, as the working mothers and children were brought into the orbit of the church, they would find ways to relate more intimately with others in the church; he had imagined something like a parent-teachers organization. But the daydream—instant community among diverse groups—made Tom cringe and groan too, for he recognized the extraordinary effort that would fall on him to build and sustain such a group, constant organizing and reminding and motivating and enabling.

Suddenly, in the new mood of "Me, too" ministry, all that was different. He was taken by surprise one day to discover that the grandmothers and the working mothers had planned to assemble one Friday afternoon for a kind of party. Having begun to feel "Me, too" about each other, largely with Tom's help, feeling the bond of shared plight and common lot, they had begun to open up to each other more and more at the beginning and end of each day. Suddenly, they wanted to be together. *They wanted to be together.* Tom marveled at each word.

Tom had struggled so long throughout his ministry to make it happen that way. As a good shepherd he had used all his skills and talents and persuasion to get *them* to *want* to *be* together. But it had never really happened. His shepherd's crook to herd the sheep—his skills and talents and persuasion—had been as debilitating as it had been enabling. It had kept people focused on him and away from each other; it had kept people resisting the crook and herding; it had kept people from exploring and testing what *they* wanted and could do. "Imposed community" is a contradiction in terms; but how else to achieve community, or any other goal of ministry, than by managing to become an imposing minister? In his new style Tom was not abdicating ministry and leaving people on their own. Quite the opposite: He was entering into the people's lives and into ministry in a far more effective, though far less obtrusive way. He was only abandoning his crook and his herding role. He was abandoning, with a wrench, to be sure, the most visible and most popular signs of ministry. After the women began meeting in genuine community, no one (not even Tom) thought to say that he had got them together. They wanted to be together. He had not made them get together. He had done that which made them *want* to get together and able to *be* together.

At the day-care center hair never did get combed much better, and tardiness was still common. But the grandmothers and working mothers were now very much in a collaborative enterprise where these things didn't matter very much. They lingered and talked to each other and brought each other to their homes, but this physical intimacy was not nearly so important as the spiritual intimacy that developed. When they looked at each other, even when wordlessly transferring children, they felt a bond and not a barrier. But the bond had been discovered by looking within the barriers as they were deeply and painfully felt.

Tom gave up a lot when he found his ministry transformed. He had felt required to be a good shepherd, strong, committed, effective, giving the kind of help that people needed. All ministers are so called and want to respond; it is the very power of that call and the vigor of our commitment to respond to it that besets us. We want to respond, but find we can't; we lack the wisdom or the strength or the circumstances. Our call is frustrated and with it our sense of our strength and our competence and our commitment. In our frustration everything in us wants to cling to that call, to reaffirm our strength, to reclaim and recall others to their role in our call as objects or as partners in our helping. We often need others to be these lost sheep and want to insist that they be so, so that we can remain the strong, wise good shepherd. It takes special grace to admit one's own lostness and to heed the new leading, new call, new roles, especially when one's intentions are thwarted, especially when the call on which one has lodged so much identity is blocked. This is the grace that Tom Goddard felt that enabled him to look so squarely into the frustration as his day-care center project floundered. This is the grace that Tom managed to communicate to the grandmothers that enabled them to experience their lostness enough to feel found again.

# PART FOUR

**present**, v. 1. being at the speci-
fied or understood place; at hand;
in attendance; opposed to *absent*.
2. existing or happening now; in
process. n. 1. the present time. 2.
the present occasion. v.t. 1. to put
before (someone), present, offer,
hence a gift. 2. to bring (a person)
into the presence of another or
others. 3. to offer to view or notice. 4. to offer for consideration.
5. to offer for acceptance; make a
gift of; bestow. 6. to point, level,
or aim, as a weapon.

# The Presence
# of Ministry

# 13

# Joseph: Called into Service

*Then Joseph got up, took the child and his mother by night, and went to Egypt.*

Matthew 2:14

*Joseph gave them wagons according to the instruction of Pharaoh, and he gave them provisions for the journey.*

Genesis 45:21b

*After these things, Joseph of Arimathaea, who was a disciple of Jesus...asked Pilate to let him take away the body of Jesus. Pilate gave him permission; so he came and removed his body.*

John 19:38

He was, apparently, a man who loved to be at home. But all we know of him is his life as a pilgrim, an exile, a refugee. He intended and deserved wife, children, and settled homestead. But his wife had prior claims on her, his son was not his son, and he lived his life on the run—trekking to Bethlehem at the behest of an emperor, fleeing to an alien land to escape one vengeful king, and taking up permanent exile to evade another. His dreams of marriage and family and homestead, just because he took them seriously, embroiled him in an eerie drama of virgin birth and God-come-to-earth and in a bloody rivalry with a ruling king.

We *want* for Joseph—as we want for ourselves—to be settled a householder. So we invent for him—as we invent for ourselves—scenes of Joseph surrounded by children, Joseph contented and industrious in his carpentry shop, Joseph manfully and tenderly training his son in his craft, Joseph esteemed among the village elders, Joseph the solid citizen, Joseph the model "man." But all we *know* is of Joseph on the run,

Joseph on the verge of the settled life, Joseph in the wilderness. Not the dramatic, unmistakable Moses-wilderness of manna and tablets and assurance of a promised land. Not the dramatic, unmistakable John-the-Baptist-wilderness of furious call to repentance and heaven-splitting baptism. Not the dramatic, unmistakable Jesus-wilderness of confrontation with demonic temptation. Just a man's lifelong, unheroic, unheralded wilderness; just a man drab and displaced, sidelined, sand-trapped, sand-bagged. Not the wilderness that is encountered en route to a promised land, but a wilderness that is off course, off the route, and a traveler who is uprooted, an exile from the land promised and yearned for, not a pilgrim marching toward it.

That's the Joseph story. That's a minister's story: promises hijacked, life diverted, trapped in dreams too big or chores too mean. Dreams too big and chores too mean and the excruciating way that dreams become chores.

Trapped by our desperate hunger for the promises to be true, we fiercely latch onto the pieces of the promises that we can reach, and the imitations, and take the part for the whole, the role for the reality, the idol for the god, the empty yes for the hearty yes, the masked yes for the almost yes, compulsive one-up-ness for genuine loftiness, the other's script as our own destiny, their errands as our life.

Trapped by the urgency of our own dreaming, we try so hard to force the dreams to come true, to patch broken dreams, to make things happen our way, that we lock ourselves into the self-imposed chores of freezing, crippling, rolling the stone uphill. Our very yearning for the promised land poisons itself, hijacks us into exile. The birthright of life that surges within our call gets thwarted by the scripts fashioned to make us "ministers."

How to find new life within the predicament, to reclaim the predicament and to make it serve us, not vice versa? What newness can our diverted dreams and diverting chores yield to us?

Joseph did it, Joseph of Nazareth and Joseph of Canaan. Men who would be doers, they got distracted by dreams—their principal encounters were with beings of the night—and then found in them vigorous mission. Men who cherished abode, both were driven into exile in Egypt, then in the very exile found themselves newly grounded and located. In their displacement, they found enduring place. If Joseph had known life as he—and we—most wanted it, we would never have known Joseph. It is the difference between surrendering to the exiling drudgery, letting it own you, and claiming it, living it so vigorously and deliberately that you own it.

In exile, in any of its forms, what are the choices? One: to escape, to defy, to repudiate the claims on you; they do not provide the structures of your life. Two: to surrender, to accept the claims on you, as though they are, after all, your destiny. Or, there is a third way: You may think I am going to suggest something halfway between escape and surrender. But I don't think such timid temporizing is possible; there is no halfway. These are the only genuine responses, to fight or to join. The third way, I think, is to do both, simultaneously: renounce *and* surrender. Play our role heartily, as though it were the real thing, and disdain it with a hearty horse laugh, knowing it isn't. You may be in a role now, thoroughly playing it out, but you are not the role. You may own it, but it doesn't own you. Accept the script, but know you are more than any script. Live out the looseness and freedom of hearty overcommitment.

The dreams of the night. The drudgery of chores. Two huge distractions in which Joseph—every Joseph—finds call; no, loses call; no, finds call. First, a minister claims ministry through taking control, managing deliberately and self-consciously, planning the daily schedule, planning the long career. Then a minister loses call by losing control in submission to dreams, in submission to tedious chores—Joseph's two forms of exile—and perhaps also, for other Josephs, in emotional outburst and violence, or in relentless ennui. Dreams and chores (or violence or ennui) happen *to* him; they take over; they distract him from his destiny. Dreams and chores sideline Joseph, put him out of the action. He loses control—and thereby loses himself. He loses control over his goals, his daily goals and his life goals, and over the means of achieving them. When dreams and chores take over, the person disappears, swallowed up. Ministers grieve, and for good reason, at the end of an hour surrendered, in spite of themselves and their best planning, to distracting daydreaming or to distracting busywork; at the end of a day or the end of a week that is "shot"; at the end of a life, or midway through it, when they suddenly, sometimes violently, sometimes in the "burnout" of ennui, look up to discover themselves in exile far from their promised land, hijacked by dreaming and drudgery never owned, barely acknowledged, just passively done.

But not Joseph, either Joseph. A doer, deflected into obedience to dreams and to the chores assigned him, he didn't fight, he switched. He didn't just tolerate his distractions, he lived vigorously and thoroughly into them. Like the other "wise men" who, steadfastly and far from home, followed their distraction, a wayward star, Joseph gave his all—a surrender of sorts, but an assertive, claiming surrender—to these unexpected, unwelcome intrusions into his plans, just as though distractions conveyed meaning and destiny. And they did. They intruded. They undid him. They turned his life around. They put him in touch with a new destiny, undreamed of. And he claimed it.

The dreamer and the chore boy are such different figures, the one with his mind wafted away, eyes closed, oblivious to the present, the other with mind numbed, eyes glazed, and preoccupied with the immediate; the one relaxed and loose, the other fixed and bent; one in flights of fancy, racing into the unfamiliar, attention leaping up and out and away, the other plodding among the all-too-familiar, facing down and inward and backward. The dreamer and the chore boy are both "spaced out," on opposite sides of normal daily life. But Joseph is both, Joseph of Canaan, Joseph of Nazareth, Joseph of today. Joseph moves readily from one to the other, from dreaming into chores, from drudgery into dreams. For Joseph has discovered that, despite their differences, dreaming and drudgery are one. They are two forms of alienation from life, two forms of discovery and reflection about life, two forms of catapulting into life. Each gives the mind a massage but also a message.

Daydreams, night dreams, superstitious habits, intuitive hunches, idealistic commitments, alcoholic binges, bizarre movies, science fiction; tedious, monotonous chores, such as mowing the grass or sitting through committee meetings or yielding to the numbing rituals of church politics—all the fixed and fixing scripts—these things, dreams and chores, make you feel out of it, dazed, estranged and alienated, somehow captured or drugged. Giving in to dreams or giving in to chores, you lose control, lose autonomy; you feel somehow under control of another, and you are. Something alien is carrying you along and away. These are mindless moments, usual vigilance and control relaxed. They are automatic, that is, *self*-acting; they enact themselves; they enact us. We do not enact the moments. The dream dreams us; the task tasks us.

Yet exactly because they *are* mindless moments, dreams and chores are moments of message. Yielding control, our usual conscious control, we are ready to receive, to hear from those lively parts of the self that are ordinarily neglected under the frozen dominion of daily self-control. The automatic moments are indeed self-making moments, moments when our fuller self, the unfrozen parts of the self, comes forth to be heard and seen. When it feels automatic, it is the self acting, the self taking charge, showing itself, in the absence of that constant vigilance and monitoring and shaping, which is really an obedience to others. When we go on automatic we are able to set aside, for the time being—truly a time for being—that preoccupation with the expectations of others. In our daily occupation at best, we occupy ourselves. We inhabit fully our own lives. We possess ourselves.

Self-consciousness is eased off, and the self surges up, those parts of the self hidden and neglected most of the time when life is under the rule of those timid, earnest monitors—the adolescent self-consciousness—peering back over the shoulder and squinting about, watchfully shaping life to the images of others. In routines, as in dreams, the self's own images stand forth, to be discerned and joined by those who will. The earnest, timid self-containing coach of self-consciousness wants to dismiss dreams and drudgery as trivial and their disclosures as meaningless. But the daily chores are the fundamental rituals of life by which the wisdom of the race and the character of the self and the call of the Creator are discovered and contoured and transmitted and celebrated. It has been in the mindless doings of plowing and spinning, caravaning across the desert and sailing the seas, marching in formation and splitting wood—rituals of work as mindless and powerful as rituals of worship or of sex—that people have always discovered and confirmed the most significant things about themselves. It was to Mary at her chores and the shepherds at their chores that the news came, and to Joseph as attentive, fussing husband, and to the other Joseph as errand boy for his father and as dutiful steward to Potiphar and as conscientious trusty in jail and as bureaucratic governor. The most discerning of our friends, and the most discerning part of ourselves, listens patiently to our well-chosen, well-controlled words and then says, "What you are doing speaks more loudly about who you are than what you are saying."

Though our routines may seem dreary and peripheral to what our fantasies would like our life to be, our routines are nevertheless the rootings, the routings by which we are enrolled, entranced into life, called into service. Our lives are grounded and lived out in daily routines just as mean and just as glorious, just as meaningless and just as revealing as—and because of—God's outrageous, squandering dive into the squalid, mean, humdrum routines of daily human life. If God is best disclosed by looking squarely at the dramatically undramatic life of Jesus, by looking squarely at, not away from, the grindings of history and the mean clashes and clatter of daily news, inside pages as much as front page, then each of us may best discover ourselves by attending to the daily drudgery, the mindless drudgery of our own rooting routine, with as much awe as to our soaring dreams.

To be Joseph is to risk taking dreams seriously, to choose to live into dreams, to choose to live by dreams, to choose to be lived by them, not shrinking from their disastrous consequences, right up to the dreary chores or pit or exile; then to choose to persist living into, living by, being lived by, these assignments, until they reap their new harvest of startling, unwelcome, life-displacing, life-giving dreams.

To be Joseph is to dream of a scientific theorem so fanciful that it accounts for all the atoms and all the stars, to announce that theory as boldly and as naïvely as Joseph disclosed his dreams to his brothers, to set one's life by the dream totally—knowing all the while that the more intensely you commit yourself to it and advertise it, the more readily and the more surely you will find yourself exiled and mocked for a dream disproved. You welcome the exile as the necessary condition for the dreaming of new dreams. Only in exile in Egypt is there dream and assurance of new homeland for Joseph and Mary; only in exile in Egypt is there the reassembling of family for Joseph and his brothers.

To be Joseph is to be a carpenter obeying the dream to create with your own hands lovely furniture and gracious interiors; to live that dream so obediently that your business grows and grows until you are exiled from carpentry and spend all your time managing finance, marketing, personnel, and large administrative machinery; then to discover that in this exile there is a new dream, a new destiny—discovered only when the exile is lived as intensely as the first dream—now the vision of creating community, work teams, a coalition of woodworkers; you become skilled at and fulfilled from the art of fitting people with each other and fitting people with their work, and you find as much beauty in the psychic work space you create as in the dens you once paneled and furnished, now designing your own interiors and not others'.

To be Joseph is to dream of becoming a professor and to live that dream intently until appointment and tenure are in hand, only to discover that the professional role is so straitened as to be an exile of drudgery: Students and public expect you to pronounce and to profess, not just search and query; the university expects you to chair committees; the politics of academia requires you to connive; publishers require you to shape your ideas to market needs. The dream has led you into exile from itself. But in that exile there is ferment and newness—so long as the exiled role is lived in as fully to the breaking point as was the dream—and discovery of hitherto undreamed ways of shaping ideas and moving students, new ways of being the professor by a forced breaking out of the role of professor.

To be Joseph is to invest, at high risk, everything—money, time, passion—into your business because your dream so compels you, to be tiptoeing constantly on the thin edge, the narrow ridge, daily risking the loss of all in exile, in bankruptcy, as the only way to gain.

To be Joseph is to be drawn, dreamed, by the personal pain surrounding you to become a counselor, to re-vision and reshape people's lives—only to discover that you don't counsel, but you listen; you don't reshape, but you mirror the misshapes; you can't change people, only stand by. But in this exile of decidedly not intervening and rearranging and reshaping people's lives, of decidedly not healing their pain, of decidedly not redirecting their priorities, you find yourself providing the necessary conditions—and so you are doing it after all—that enable them to do just such re-visioning and reshaping.

To be Joseph is to be called by dreams to minister to a community of the faithful only to be called as the minister of a particular church of people of decidedly ambiguous faith and commitment, people who leave you stranded time after time after time in the role of lonely champion of justice and mercy and faithfulness to God; only to discover that when you leave that lonely championship role, when you yield your call to be representative for God, when you leave that all behind and join the people where they are, in exile from God and from ministry and from faithfulness of community, when you join that community of exile intensely and fully and honestly, there is a new, undreamed-of transaction between God and people, flowing through your very exile of faithlessness.

To be Joseph is to get appointed, at last, to the committee of your dreams, in your city, your church, your club, or wherever, the committee of power and decision—the executive committee, the membership committee, the finance committee, whatever. Now: power and influence and a real use of your vision and wisdom. Out of the muddy road where you have been spinning your wheels, and onto the superhighway. Inside the Holy of Holies. You read background papers, you anticipate the issues and prepare your positions. You compose speeches in your head. You build personal rapport with the other committee members. Your wisdom and commitment to the committee and its mission are so evident that you know that soon this wisdom and commitment will be fully engaged and widely appreciated. You live fully into the dreams and the glorious future to which it points.

Then, Joseph, your very forwardness and intensity—the dream itself and your commitment to it—sabotage the dream. It—you—turn people off and push them away. Your earnestness runs afoul of the sluggishness of the committee, and the sluggishness fouls your earnestness. It turns out that the committee, any committee, has an earnest, relentless, deadly life of its own; to be a member of the committee, to be committed to the committee, is to join this deadly routine. The more you are committed to the committee, the more you get ground into this inertia and your dreams get ground down by it. It's a whole new world, Joseph. The new committee—or new job, new school, any new setting for your dreams—has its own culture, its own history, its own language, its own earnest rituals, this Egypt into which your dreams have led you, this pit, this stable. Your ideals and your speeches don't fit here. This world doesn't move by ideals and speeches, but by subtle political processes and signals. The decisions somehow are all made out of sight. You are Alice dropped down into the rabbit hole, through the looking glass, into a world with exotic logic. Some things are circuitous and delayed and meandering, and other things happen even before you know it in ways you do not recognize. It just doesn't fit. It must be like God walking among the new creation, full of dismay and wonder and intrigue.

But then, as with God, the very fact that this new culture is unfamiliar and therefore frustrating, leading dreams into exile, makes it inviting and challenging: new raw materials to create with, once you get the hang of them, frustrating tedium until you do, then gradually more entrancing. You submit to the stubborn, intransigent, frustrating stuff of this new,

175

alien, inviting world; you learn from it, and gradually it submits to you. You adapt to this once-alien ecological niche. And so, Joseph, you find yourself, after a wandering exile, speaking the new language of the committee, caucusing and patiently waiting out routines and signaling political compromise in the private code language of the committee. It is all very different from your dreams of power, but not so different after all, a natural evolution. It still turns out that you are making things happen—as Joseph dreamed from the beginning. You are doing your thing their way.

To be Joseph is to be God struggling to transform dream into creation, creation into dream, an act that is possible only at the risk of trusting that creation, an act that is stymied and betrayed by the risk of trusting that creation, for the creation betrays the dream and lurches into self-exile, out the gates of Eden, over and over and over again. God struggles from the mountaintop, the place of the gods, to make things right, but the betrayal goes on until finally God gives up. God gives up all, God surrenders Godship, becomes self-exiled from heaven, and eventually even from life, in manger and on a cross and all the homelessness and humiliation in between, a grand exile, which welds creation and dream.

To be Joseph is to be any author, like God, yearning urgently to form into words, words of flesh and blood, the aspirations and wisdom that loom so insistently but mistily in the corners of the mind: how to bring into being—how to make the word become flesh—how to interpret the dreams—how to imagine life. And the author is constantly caught in a web of drudgery, an exile that defies the dreams far more than it gives them lodging, but a drudgery and exile that is somehow a necessary and fruitful sojourn and that finally yields up, when the struggle is abandoned—sometimes in the dreams of the night—the words and the metaphors that give life after all to the dreams, give text to a call, give image to life, at least for the moment.

# 14

## Modern Josephs: A Powerful Sense of Presence

*"Those who try to make their life secure will lose it, but those who lose their life will keep it."*

Luke 17:33

177

As this is being written, Isaac Bashevis Singer is dead, the Yiddish storyteller of powerful and authentic emotions because he was a storyteller of simple people and simple deeds, a protector and nourisher of the self because he insisted on a certain heedlessness of the self. To name his power, his obituaries and his admirers resort to the word *childlike*. He retained, they say—*retrieved* might be the better word—the wonder and the terror of a child. He saw things unsmoothed and untempered by adult wisdom (eulogizing a naïveté we honor in adults more than in children, whom we hurry along into precocity). Like a child not daring or not permitted to wander too far from home, he chose to limit his world, the world of his daily routines and the world of his storytelling, to a few blocks of Broadway and to the villages and ghettos of his childhood, which the neighborhood recalled for him; but to limit meant to hone and to probe. Prowling Broadway coffee shops for the perfect rice pudding had for him, like one of his own characters, an urgency and ultimacy unrisked by the adult on the trail of grown-up grails. He was the child who could call the strutting emperor (especially, perhaps, the imperious claim of intellectual pretensions) naked, but more, could name the fool wise, and the plain rich. Receiving a Nobel Prize in a formal ceremony, he could be true, and speak true, only by lapsing into Yiddish.

But *childlike* seems not quite right, at least not to be taken literally. I. B. Singer's simplicity is not regression but is a maturing, a renunciation that is a transcendence, a finding that comes *after* possessing and relinquishing, not before, a selfhood that is beyond selfhood, like the plain rivers and trees at the end of the Zen journey, not at its beginning. He models a selfhood that has encountered more than one man's quota of adversities but has neutralized them and absorbed their power, like the martial art of turning the attacker's energy to your benefit. Forced into confinement and estrangement by history and temperament, he chose to make the confinement a flourishing homestead, his exile a homeland. What can we learn from Singer about selfhood thriving in endangerment by paring down to impregnable essentials, about finding oneself by losing it?

Is it the same we can learn from other models and teachers? What about Carl Rogers, the "non-directive" psychotherapist (and maybe Fred, the one with the TV neighborhood), or what about Mohandas K. Gandhi, the "non-violent" liberator of India?

Gandhi is another who was denied conventional badges of selfhood by history and temperament, yet who displayed in that denial an unconventional and enhanced selfhood. Scorned at every turn by the self-certifying authorities from train conductors, who refused to honor his first-class ticket, to the British Empire, and even the chiefs of his own caste, Gandhi found fierce power in renouncing all they held dear and demanded from him. Self-stripped of possessions, of institutional power in any conventional sense, without worldly uniform or costume, virtually without clothes at all, and puny of body, without a "nice" personality or negotiating charm, Gandhi made this nakedness of power an icon of power and the principle of renunciation a foundation. He displayed a kind of raw selfhood that had a stark presence and power that transcended that of conventional badges of selfhood, a raw selfhood matching the common everyday starkness of symbols, such as salt and spinning, that he deployed. Refusing to meet adversaries on their terms of conventional strength, he made them meet him in his unconventional simplicity, a weakness turned into power. He refused to bargain with mill owners or British rulers in their fashion, but required them, while they trembled, to drink tea with him. The humiliating third-class railroad car became an icon of power, his triumphant funeral cortege. The government of the British Empire came to a virtual standstill while it waited for Gandhi to sip from a glass of orange juice. As for the power of his caste rulers, he made caste irrelevant. Dressed sometimes like a baby, preoccupied, it often seemed, with oral needs, and following strategies that could be likened to infantile temper tantrums, Gandhi too could be called childlike, or even childish. But that would be to misunderstand as regressive what was transcending. His power is a developed power, developed out of renouncing power, a selfhood beyond selfhood. How do we understand it; how do we appropriate it?

What is the therapeutic power of Carl Rogers, and how is it achieved? What selfhood does he portray in a "client-centered" therapeutic hour? The caricatures are right, or half-right: He seems a nonentity, mechanically parroting the client, bland. The things that we usually suppose make for personality and a sense of self-presence are absent—sociability, opinions and attitudes, feelings, and history. Watching him on film or in person, one has a sure sense that, if interrupted during a therapy hour and asked his name, he couldn't answer easily, so radically other-directed is this "nondirective" therapist, so totally abdicating of his distinctiveness and so engrossed in the other, so oblivious to the boundaries that construct and define the self. One does not leave Carl Rogers the therapist with the sense of having had a conversation with another person. But there is also a powerful sense of presence. A client, or an observer, has no doubt about having experienced an indelible personality, one who is decisively other even while—or because— strangely merged. Stripped of the conventional characteristics of personality, Rogers emerges with a raw selfhood, an intense, primitive, generic presence, a kind of ahistorical, asocial, arelational selfhood in a world that is used to defining selfhood in historical, social, relational terms.

Singer, Gandhi, Rogers: Whence the power and presence they fashion; how can they move and heal as they do? A mostly sociological answer comes first to mind, then yields to a mostly theological answer.

Sociologically (or perhaps, anti-sociologically): Culture scripts and conscripts us with expectations and roles that serve it and its institutions, but distort the self, which is to be conceived as fundamentally autonomous and as most genuine when it can shake free from the oppressive socialization. Singer, Gandhi, and Rogers summon us, and themselves (and in Gandhi's case, a nation) to selfhood by excavating through the socially acquired debris in order to display the autonomous self. But this conventional social-psychological diagnosis, though perhaps true and important, seems relatively trite, 1960s-ish, perhaps a little adolescent (or belonging to the mid-life crisis stage of adolescence), and not too interesting. It smacks of the liberal optimism that the perils to the self are historical or accidental and remediable.

Singer, Gandhi, Rogers have their power for reasons more fundamental and more radical than declaration of independence from social conventions and constraints. Beyond this liberal, social-psychological diagnosis, the power of self-assertion, they display the power of self-renunciation. They illustrate that there is something about the *act of yielding* that is itself transformative, transcendent. Is not the seed dying in the ground to create life a fundamental revelation? Is not the universe—existence—constructed so that life issues out of death, so that we do not fully participate in life, we are left on the margins, we are not in touch with the throb, the fact of life, except we enact surrender, death?

Is this not the common denominator of religious urging and promise (following certainly the lessons of tides and seasons, of night and day, of breathing out in order to breathe in)? Access to transcendent and transforming power is via the postures and rhythms of sacrifice, vulnerability, surrender, martyrdom, relinquishment, the death that is required/symbolized in conversion, initiation, baptism, circumcision, in the postures of prayer, meditation, the self-denial of bowing and confession. Access to life is through death.

In this case, what is intrinsically empowering is not that Singer, Gandhi, and Rogers renounce *culturally* defined characteristics of selfhood (for the sake of some culture-free self). What *is* empowering is that they renounce *whatever* characteristics they (and their cultures) really do rely on. They must genuinely renounce a meaningful and attractive selfhood—which may well be a socially learned and endorsed self. Losing the self (to find the self) works only when the renounced self is a first-class, primary self, not a second-class or derived self. The emptying of self that is empowering and defining of self is inherent, an end in itself, not instrumental; it is not that one strips away the husk to get the kernels known to exist inside, winnows the chaff to get at the known grain; one yields *all*.

So it may be that Singer, Gandhi, and Rogers, in their emptying and renunciation, witness to us and we witness in them testimony to the way things are and the way we are, alluring and frightening testimony.

# Afterword

The first course paper I wrote as a seminary student—exactly fifty years ago—was a modest and makeshift research project, interviewing a dozen of my classmates about the circumstances or call that brought them to a seminary. I was curious, intrigued, awestruck, that people would voluntarily enter a vocation that promised inevitable disappointments, that they would be lured by hopes and dreams right into a trap so obviously poised to thwart the very hopes and dreams it abetted. Fifty years later, a couple of thousand divinity students later, a couple of dozen clergy workshops later, several more formal research projects later, a dozen books later, I remain amazed that men and women are still lured, sometimes in joy, sometimes in anguish, by a calling that yields such pain to the soul.

Assembling these chapters in one place makes vivid that the lens I have kept on ministry has been monotonously focused on these disappointments. It also makes clear, I hope, my conviction that these griefs are ultimately important not because they are challenges of call but because they are custodians of call.

These chapters beat out an incessant inventory of pains that beset Christian ministry: Ministers are isolated, called to tasks for which they are unready, serving among people who are even more unready, people who misunderstand not just their sermons but their mission, people who lay on ministry their own inflated or demeaning demands. Ministers are seduced and betrayed, their call and commitment deflected and smothered by chores and conflicts, effectiveness found only in surrender of dreams and status. In a phrase Donald Capps lifts up in his generous foreword, ministry, if it is truly ministry, is not part of any working ecology. It has no niche.

It remains here to acknowledge, indeed to claim, even to celebrate this preoccupation with the persistent and painful mis-fitness of ministry and to make very clear that this preoccupation is intended as a theological affirmation, a statement of faith. This exploration of the griefs of ministry is not intended primarily as pastoral care of ministers, to dress their wounds. It is not intended as a call to institutional reform and remedy, to redress the wrongs. Quite the opposite. These chapters portray my understanding of how ministry is *intended* to be, a chronic misfit, comfortable resident of neither heaven nor earth because committed—like the persistent God who calls us—to reconcile these ir-reconcilable domains. I would claim my depiction of ministry to be "realistic"—not in the dualistic sense that we must balance ministry's high ideals by facing its morbid and sordid underside, but in the oppo-site, holistic sense that what we see here is the *essence of ministry*. The griefs are not just regrettable side effects of ministry or wasteful by-products or avoidable contingencies. They are inevitable because they are inherent. They are what make ministry ministry.

What is it underlies and structures these assembled chapters? I think it is this: Ministry is a sacrament.

Whether or not all church councils have said so, ministry is a sacra-ment. It is a bridge between the transcendent and the temporal, anchored securely in both but resident in neither, chronic misfit in both. Ministry is a bridge between life as it is lived and life as it is intended and prom-ised, between the drudgery and the dreams. Ministry is a go-between and belongs in the between-ness, in the disparateness, the dissonance. It loses its reason for being if it tries to settle in the temporal (by striving, for example, for "relevance" or social acceptance) or if it tries to settle in the transcendent (in biblical literalism, for example, or moral absolutes, or liturgical proficiency). God has made the commitment to inhabit this between-ness, this no-man's-land, this no-God's-land, and so does God's ministry.

Ministry is a sacrament. That means that the ordinary daily routine of one's vocation—like the ordinary foodstuffs of bread and wine—is appointed to convey the presence of the transcendent. That which is not holy conveys holiness. That which is mortal and finite conveys the Eter-nal. That which is not (yet) part of the kingdom conveys access to the kingdom. That which is flawed and faithless conveys the promises of God. That which is highly conditioned conveys the impact of the absolute.

Such a commission destines the minister to an identity crisis that is chronic, inevitable, perpetual, and defining of the call. The minister's identity crisis echoes the anguished deliberations the church has given to identifying the nature of the sacraments at the altar: What *is* the bread and the wine? It is ordinary *and* it is extraordinary, it is earthly *and* it is holy, it is the meanest stuff of life *and* it is transcendent. The minister's identity crisis echoes the anguished deliberation the church has given to the identity of Christ: How can one be both human and godly?

Ministry is a sacrament. That means that ministry is caught squarely in the middle of the fundamental religious dilemma and aspiration. How can heaven and earth meet, yet remain heaven and earth, not compromise or obliterate each other like a collision of matter and antimatter? To be saved, the human race needs to be reached by the transcendent, yet the transcendent must not be compromised by the encounter, must remain

183

transcendent—or there is no saving. And, too, humanity must be saved *in* its humanity and not transposed into some quasi-transcendence (as perhaps in puritanic or ascetic or mystic excess, for example)—destroying the village to save it, as it were (as literally happens when cults resort to death pacts as their mechanism of saving)—or there is no genuine saving. In Jesus' metaphor, how can we acquire the childlikeness that is prerequisite for the kingdom without sacrificing hard-won adult maturity of faith? Ministry finds itself at the point of this paradox, as God finds self, fully incarnating human life yet maintaining aloof transcendence from it, fully acknowledging transcendence yet sharing the divine imperative to commit this transcendence to the benefit of the world. It is hardly surprising that ministry is isolated or misunderstood.

Ministry is a sacrament. As such, it must convey fully the transcendent yet point beyond itself to a genuine transcendent that cannot be contained or limited or even fully known. So mystery always attends a sacrament, and a commitment—which I was once taught to identify as the "Protestant principle"—to advertising its own boundaries, its own finiteness, its own incompleteness, its own failure. Ministry is *meant* to be disillusioning, just as these chapters have described it.

That is, sacraments are to avoid becoming idols, worshiped and trusted for themselves, not for what they point to beyond themselves. Yet sacraments inevitably do become idols, the sacrament of ministry foremost among them. In grand councils of the church and in petty parish bickering and in inevitable human posturing by ministers, particular habits and structures and styles of ministry are absolutized. Yet this suggests one final paradox: Perhaps the most faithful way of using a sacrament to testify to that which transcends it is to invest heavily in it, to treat it as though absolute, to idolize it, until it self-destructs of its own weight and reveals in its destruction that which transcends it. Idols, like the golden calf, are destined to be crumbled and consumed, and in that process to leave opening for new revelation and commitment, fresh discernment and a new, daring venture at approximating access to God through new sacrament. Ministers may be most faithful in pursuing energetically their particular approximations of ministry, pursuing them single-mindedly to the breaking point, knowing that they *will* break, and knowing too that in that breaking God awaits with renewed call.

James E. Dittes